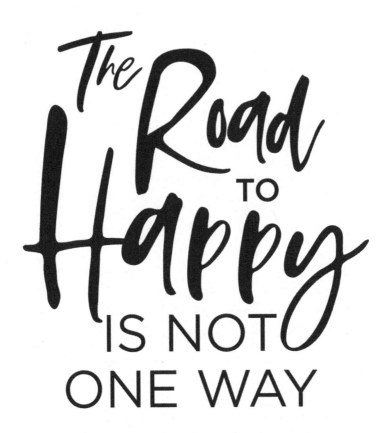

The Road to Happy IS NOT ONE WAY

Seven Essential Principles
and a Guided Workbook to
**Help You Keep Driving Toward
Everyday Happiness**

SARA GLASHAGEL

ISBN Hardback: 978-1-7372617-0-4
ISBN Paperback: 978-1-7372617-1-1

To Cameron, Chloe, and Olivia

While I may have brought each of you into this world, after living thirty of my years without you, it was YOU who gave ME life. I'll never be able to put into words how special you are to me. I will continue to spend the rest of my life trying to make you proud, and I will always strive to teach you the importance of honesty, integrity, and acceptance. You are each so kind and loving already, and I am so proud of you.

Love, Mom

TABLE OF CONTENTS

PREFACE

Before you decide to take the advice of some mom in Midwest suburbia, maybe I should tell you what makes me so all-knowing when it comes to tragedy, trauma, drowning in mental illness, and then ultimately climbing my way out of it. So before I start dishing out advice, I think I need to establish a little credibility here, and to do that, I need to go back to the beginning.

Because here's the thing, if you look at me on the surface now, you might say, "Damn, she's got it made!" Or, quite honestly, you could easily look at me and think, "That girl is living the absolute dream." So yes, let me start by confirming some of these very real truths and assumptions. Is my life a bit dreamy now? Sure. When I think of where I am at right at this exact moment, I would say it's overall almost identical to what I pictured one way or another when I was growing up and imagined what my adulthood would once look like.

Let me confirm here and now before I dive into my story. Yes, I am, for all intents and purposes, living an incredibly happy life. I have been married for ten years to a man I still adore, am still fully in love with, and still consider my best friend and partner in life. We have three beautiful and seemingly perfect children—seemingly being the operative word here, and I'm sure all parents know exactly what I mean. They are currently ages six, four, and one years old, and they are healthy, happy, generally well-behaved, and thriving in every way in their childhood.

My husband, Brian, and I met in 2007, began dating in 2009, and got married in 2011. We live in a northern suburb of Chicago, with all of our immediate family on both sides living within an hour of us. He and I each are very close with our parents, siblings, and extended families. Family is a huge pillar of our life, and we spend a tremendous amount of time with them. In addition to that, we have been fortunate enough to establish an extremely close group of friends who we see daily, confide in and trust, and are raising our children with them, as well.

We both work full-time in careers that are well matched for our individual passions. I am a professional photographer and own my own business. In the nearly seven years of owning my business, it has become delightfully successful and grew well beyond any expectations I ever had when I initially started it. I also work full-time at a company I absolutely adore, helping other individuals write and publish their books. I can honestly say that I have found myself, in both careers, working because I genuinely love it and not at all because I have to.

Brian is a high school teacher and head football and track coach at the high school in our town. Since the day he left college, he has been coaching; I'll brag on him for a second and say that he is truly amazing at what he does in running the entire team and organization. He also genuinely loves what he does for a living.

As annoying as kids can be, our kids are just becoming these incredible, overall good human beings. Brian and I work hard as a team to raise them to be kind, honest, respectful, and well-rounded people. That's an entire book on its own, but I think we are doing okay so far. Cameron is our oldest and was born in 2014; Chloe is our middle and was born in 2016; and Olivia, coined our Livie, was born in 2019. All of the kids are super involved in sports, activities, and have grown up with a life of constant play dates and neighborhood gatherings.

It is safe to say that we have completely established ourselves in this little world we've created for our family. We live in a nice neighborhood, are financially comfortable, go on vacations, host lots of parties and events, and are both engaged and active in our children's school and activities. So yes, when you look at my life, is it pretty close to perfect? Well, sure. One could absolutely argue that. How can you deny some of these facts and how we live? You really can't.

If someone asked me today, "What would you change in your life to make you happier?" I don't have a solid answer. Are there things that I may want that I don't have in life, like some materialistic items? Sure. I will be the first to admit that I really like nice things. Big, fancy car and house, brand new wardrobe with designer clothes anytime I want? Yes, please! I would take it. But I know, without a shadow of a doubt, that in my life right now, I am lucky beyond measure and have everything I need to be happy, and I truly am.

But here's the giant catch, and here's where I now get to prove to you my credibility that my story is far from perfect—it wasn't until about a decade ago that I even had hopes of this life I am now leading.

Where I am now, and the happiness I have fought for and continue fighting for in my life did not come easily. My life was not handed to me on a silver platter. Even though this white, suburban mom may have my act mostly together now, that was not always the case.

My trauma and mental illness story starts long before any husband, kids, or career were in the picture. I came from a broken home, but I didn't always know that this was the case. I grew up in a town that's just about thirty minutes south of where I live now. Just like the one I currently live in, it was an upper-middle-class town where we lived very comfortably. My mom, dad, older brother, Jason, and I were very happy for most of what I can remember as a child. Just like my own children, my brother and I were both extremely involved in sports and other activities that kept my parents, Jason, and I busy on weekends and summers.

I played soccer, basketball, and ran track, sang in the choir, acted in school plays, and my family was very involved in our church throughout my entire childhood. Both of my parents worked full-time and were very engaged in everything my brother and I did with school and activities.

I can pinpoint the exact turning point in my life when everything changed. I remember the moment and conversation in time when my perfect childhood up until that point was pretty much tossed out the window, and my world looked forever different. It was the Friday afternoon after Thanksgiving in 1999, and I was sitting in my room watching TV. I couldn't tell you what I was watching, but I was only fourteen years old, so my guess is that it was some sort of teenage, dramatic series which wrapped me up and kept me locked up in my room for hours on end.

My mom knocked on my door and told me that I needed to come downstairs for a family meeting. I rolled my eyes and walked through the hall and down the stairs and saw my brother already sitting there with both parents. He is four years older than me, and I could see the annoyed look on his face, as he had just been pulled away from whatever TV show he was watching at the time too. At this time, Jason attended college and played football for the University of Wisconsin at Madison, so he typically lived about two hours away and was only home for the holiday weekend and was probably going back to school the next day.

I knew right away that this would not be a fun, "we're going on a vacation" type of family meeting. I could see it in both of my parents' faces. Something was wrong. My immediate thought was that someone died, but I didn't ask. I just sat and looked at them for a minute until Jason finally said, "Okay, let's get the show on the road. Just tell us."

My dad just stared ahead as my mom started to speak. "Guys, this is not going to be easy, and I don't have a good way of telling you this, so I am just going to come out and say it. Your dad has been using drugs for several years, and he is finally at the point of us needing to seek help. We didn't want to have to tell you this, but we now need you to know what is going on."

I had absolutely no words. Drugs? I was a super naive kid at that age, and I'll admit, I didn't even know very many types of drugs at that point, let alone would I ever imagine my own dad using any. I don't think I had ever really seen him drink up to that point.

The rest of the conversation from that point on became a total blur—a blur that started at that moment in time and became a constant in my life for the next ten years or so of my life. When I say blur, I mean I literally have a series of broken memories that I have gradually been able to piece together to recall the events that took place.

When I think back to those years now, this blur, which was later described to me as a form of post-traumatic stress disorder, made it difficult to navigate through my experiences, let alone even begin to decipher some of my memories and determine if they were real or constructed in my head over time.

These memories are in a lockbox that I have subconsciously sealed so tightly that I literally cannot even access months of my life, even if I tried. I am sure that I could get some type of hypnotherapy to access those memories, but at this point in my life, I am satisfied with recalling what I can and knowing that the rest may have been forgotten for good reason.

I also cannot explain the next few years without first stating in clear conscience that as many mistakes as my parents made in the decade or so that followed, I love them dearly. I have forgiven them for everything, and I am pleased to report that my father has been clean and sober, as I write this story, for about fifteen years. His years of drug abuse ended long before I finally regained control of my own life, and I am proud of him and his accomplishment of ongoing sobriety.

I will say it now, and I'm sure I'll say it again, I view drug addiction not as the root of a problem but as the effect of deeper issues within. As an adult, I have since learned that my dad personally struggled long before drug addiction was ever a problem. He struggled with mental health, with life circumstances, and he, like so many other addicts out there, did the best he could before turning to drugs as a coping mechanism for masking other problems that were rooted so much further within.

So anyway, back to the pivotal conversation. In a matter of seconds, the biggest problem in my world shifted from missing an episode of *Dawson's Creek* to my father, the man who had done no wrong in my eyes ever, dealing with drug addiction.

My dad, as ashamed as I had ever seen in my lifetime, was almost unable to speak to us during this talk. He was not only mortified that his children, who he loved so much, were realizing this hidden truth and his inner demons, but he was heartbroken that he was even capable of hurting his family so drastically with something like this.

My mom, immediately within this conversation, took on a new role in my life. She was no longer just the mom who attended my soccer games and school plays. She immediately became the mom whose job it was to heal me and help me through everything I was about the face. That burden was put on her whether she asked for it or not.

As a mother now, I know why she took it on head first. Yet, it was not until I became a mother that I could see the burden of protecting children from the pain and suffering in the world, even when it's within your own household.

This burden of covering everything up was met with resistance from the angsty teenager within me. Everything that followed was not just his fault. Instead, at the time, I placed blame on my mom for things as trivial as not telling us sooner, "hiding" it from us. I even got mad at my mom for the years she stayed with my dad and standing by his side, even at his worst.

Over the course of the next few years, my world slowly began to unravel into a life I didn't recognize. What should be memories of my high school years are now just a series of tragedies that didn't seem to stop. My dad lost his job, and on more times than I can count, we were awoken in the middle of the night from one of many terrible phone calls from him or someone he was with, letting us know what was happening. Even though I was a teenager, I spent many nights sleeping in my mom's bed so that she wasn't alone. The phone would ring, and all I could hear was my mom's voice of dread about what she was hearing.

The phone calls varied widely, ranging from letting us know that he was lying in an alley somewhere and had been beaten up to hearing at one point that he traded our car for drugs. Essentially that meant our car was stolen from our family. It was always unimaginable and always scary to hear the phone ring. And sometimes the nights where the phone didn't ring were even scarier.

I began waking up with night terrors of not only my dad being killed but also the rest of my family. Even though I was a teenager, I was utterly naive to the world around me. It wasn't until I started glimpsing into the world that revolved around drugs and crime that I even really imagined people living in this type of fear.

I started questioning every phone call we received at the house and every police officer I saw walking down the street. I was constantly living in a state of fear that someone was coming to tell me that my father had been killed or our house had been robbed. That safe bubble I had once known and grown up in was completely gone.

After September 11th, 2001, things took an even crazier turn when my mom lost her job due to the economic downturn and everything else that was happening in the country at the time. The company where she'd spent the entirety of her career abandoned her. She felt like her only choice was to stay within her industry, and she moved three hours away to take a job and continue to provide for her family.

This is one of those decisions that I grappled with understanding. I was a junior in high school, and my mom gave me a choice. I could move with her and go to a new school or stay and finish high school while she'd leave me alone as she worked during the weeks and then come home on the weekends. I chose to stay. I know my mom gave me this choice because she had my best interests in mind, but I quickly proved her wrong in every way.

With both parents gone most of the time, I quickly surpassed the limits of freedom that any teenager should have. I began abusing her trust by staying out all night drinking, partying, and hanging out with people who I absolutely should not have been with at the time. I went from being a freshmen three-sport athlete to a senior year no-sport athlete. I threw parties at our house, started doing drugs, and my grades went from straight A's to barely scraping by.

I recall one night, I was probably a senior in high school at the time when I was with a group of friends. My parents were both gone, and we were at a party at someone's house. I couldn't tell you whose house it was, and I'm not even sure what town we were in. I didn't know anyone who lived in the house. I was sitting at the bottom of the stairs talking to a group of friends, none of us even remotely concerned with the rules or getting in trouble. In, through the front door which sat right in front of me, walked two police officers.

My friends immediately started to scatter throughout the house to get away because they didn't want to get in trouble. However, my instinct was to stay put; I wanted to know if they'd come to tell me that my dad was dead. It set aside rational fears of getting in trouble and replaced them with worry for my own family.

In this case, the police were only there to break up the high school party. The officers asked everyone to call their parents for a ride home. Well, my parents weren't available. I couldn't call my mom, who lived three hours away, and I certainly couldn't call my dad, who was gone, and I didn't know where he was or even how to reach him.

When it came time for the officer to ask me to make the call, he asked where my parents were. I quietly asked him if he could come over to the side where nobody else could hear me; I was embarrassed that someone would find out that my parents were not home, and I told him. I explained that I had no idea how to contact my parents effectively.

I don't know if he was just having a good day or what, but the officer kindly told me to sit on the stairs and wait until everyone else had cleared out, and then he would drive me home.

The whole way home, I had a pit in my stomach. He talked to me the entire way, asking about where my dad was and how often my mom came home to visit. He was incredibly kind, giving me advice and telling me that I needed to stay away from parties and keep myself out of trouble.

I remember him saying something that I've always kept with me. He said, "You're smart. I can tell. You're too good to get in trouble at one of these stupid high school parties. You're better than this."

I clearly remember his words because it wasn't the last time I received that piece of advice. Sadly, I've heard that exact phrase uttered out of the mouths of so many people—people who saw the red flags before I did, people who saw a good kid gradually working her way into a bad world.

I thanked him for the ride home and went inside, and locked the door behind me like I always did. Alone. Seventeen years old. He was the first of many people in my life who saw and addressed a problem years before I ever would open my own eyes to it.

I dealt with living alone by doing everything in my power to make it so that nobody knew my reality. The thought of my friends knowing I was alone at night was terrifying, so I learned young how to put on a front and look happy and perfect, even though I was empty and hurting on the inside. My only goal was to graduate high school so that I could get into college and start over again from scratch.

Despite my grades drastically slipping, I made it into a great school where I suppose I was given a second chance. But it was only a matter of time before reality set in, as naturally, my past was quickly following me close behind. I remember coming into my freshman year thinking that I could now be whoever I wanted to be, and I would not let anyone know about what I was dealing with back at home.

As much as I did my best to create this perfect persona of the have-it-all girl who could get good grades and be the life of the party, I slowly started to unravel. Over my college years, and without anyone even having any idea, I developed an eating disorder and had multiple suicide attempts. I had so many run-ins with college law enforcement that at one point, I received an order of correction where I was given a 6-month probationary period where—if I warranted any type of discretionary action, I would be kicked out of my major.

I was suffering inside but never admitted it. So, my college friends instead will only remember me as the fun-loving drunk girl who loved to do crazy things at parties and wound up getting in trouble, always leading to funny stories and situations. This was the first time I remember acknowledging what feeling truly alone looked and felt like.

I remember one night, all of my friends were going out, and for some reason, I just wasn't feeling it. This was not the norm at all, as I typically took any chance I got to go out and drink and forget about whatever was whirling in my head. But I think I used some excuse of having a test to stay in.

I remember my roommates getting ready and dolled up to go to who knows what—probably to dance at some club for hours on end. I remember just listening to them laugh and talk as they were doing their hair. They sat for an hour or so, drinking and talking and laughing in the kitchen. I could hear how much fun they were having, how happy they were.

Then all of a sudden, it got quiet. They were gone. Nobody said goodbye; nobody came into my room to tell me to have a good night. They just left.

Now, I'm sure they were just having a good time, the ride came, and they raced out not to miss it, but it didn't matter.

It hit me. Did they even care that I was there? Would they have more fun tonight now that I wasn't going out? Deep down, I knew I wasn't anything like them. I didn't fit in. Maybe I acted like I did, but I knew I really didn't. When you spend most of your life as a chameleon blending into every environment, it's actually quite shocking when you take a step back and realize how different you are from those around you.

We had many serious talks about life and our futures, especially recently as we were getting close to graduation, but I still knew we were on far different pages in life. I didn't even know how to achieve that level of happiness that I could hear from them. It just wasn't in me anymore. It had been stripped out of me at some point. Through the drunken nights, somewhere the "fun Sara" was just gone. I couldn't even fake it anymore.

I felt so alone and so empty inside that I started just crying and could not stop. I must have cried for an hour. My mind started to spin and spin; the thoughts started to creep in as they had in the past. "What if I just disappeared? Would they even care? How am I ever going to afford to live on my own after college? Where will I even go? What kind of future is even out there waiting for me? I'm never going to amount to anything." The thoughts were racing and would not stop.

I then began thinking about how I could do it, how I could end it all. What was the point of staying alive? It's like that feeling when you're standing at a party, and you realize you have nobody to talk to and think, "Would anyone notice if I just left?"

I didn't do anything that night; I did not attempt to harm myself, but this was not the only night these thoughts crossed my mind. I think I thought about suicide at least once a week, every single week, within my last semester of college.

The thought of the real world terrified me. I had no idea how I was going to do it on my own. I had no family to fall back on, and with all my friends beginning their careers, the future was this black, empty hole that I couldn't even begin to envision—again, my friends never knew any of this. We made some great memories in those last few months of school. I have really fond memories of it all, but at the same time, I was lost, I was alone, and I was empty.

My parents were slowly working on their marriage. My dad, with on-again, off-again, sobriety was gradually making a little progress, and things on that front were getting better.

After graduating college, I worked as a teacher in a town near where I grew up. That was supposed to be exciting, right? I went to school for four years to obtain a degree, and then I got a pretty great job right out of college. Trying to make the most of it, I started over, yet again.

While I loved the job itself, it was the man I met there, Brian, that ultimately changed everything. We got hired the same year, and even though we didn't start dating right away, we were instant friends.

I want to say that he saw the real me from the start, not the chameleon me. Still, I hid so much of myself from him. We spent about two years as friends, then dated, and ultimately married. Even with his friendship and love, there was no magic fix for everything that had occurred in my life. Of course, he knew about my family situation, almost from the start, but there was still something just fighting deep within me that kept me shut off from really opening up and showing all of my genuine hurt, even from the man I had fallen in love with.

Eventually, reality caught up with me. Only six months into our marriage—as happy and head over heels in love as I was with Brian—at some point that I cannot even identify, I went deep into what, in retrospect, was a manic episode caused by bipolar disorder. I began having racing thoughts that would keep me up at night. I started contemplating taking my own life again, without any firm triggers to cause it. I began spiraling out of control, all while still acting seemingly normal to the average person.

Mental illness is funny like that.

I could be having severe hallucinations, and nobody would bat an eye because I knew exactly what to do or say to cover it up. But this time, it was too late. Not only did I engage in some terrible, risky, and illegal behavior and put my own life and career at risk, but I also sadly put Brian's life and career at risk.

Up until this point in my life, the term mania never existed in my brain, but in reality, it was something I'd been struggling with for the better half of a decade. It was not until I thoroughly disappointed and hurt Brian and his family with my actions that I finally realized something way deeper was going on than I ever knew or understood.

This was the first time in my life that, with Brian basically forcing me to do so, I finally sought professional help. For the very first time, after enduring so many tests that I was mentally exhausted after the appointments, I received the official diagnosis of anxiety, bipolar disorder, attention-deficit disorder, and post-traumatic stress disorder.

All of a sudden, I had this label. I had mental illness. But who was I supposed to talk to about this? Nobody else I knew had mental illness. This label was used for crazy people in movies. It wasn't a label that spoiled little rich kids from suburbia were ever given.

Of course, I wish I could say that this was the time when I shouted it all from the rooftop so that everyone finally understood. Nope. Wrong. My family knew, and Brian's family knew. That was it. How could I admit this to my friends? Well, not that I had many friends left after spiraling out of control for months at a time.

The next year or so of my life was a rollercoaster. If you've ever had to trial medicines, then you know, it does not always go easily. With each medicine I tried, it took weeks of getting my body used to it, and sometimes even longer for any effects to occur or for me to notice a difference. As much as I tried to hold it together, it was not possible. I was up, down, and all over the place.

I even had delusions which made it hard to decipher and stay in touch with reality. Have you ever experienced drinking so much that you don't remember the night before when you wake up in the morning? That is very much what a manic episode feels like. Saying things and doing things that you cannot even fathom doing in your sane mind, but then when you come back to reality, all of a sudden, you have to explain what just happened.

While I thought that just because I avoided the tragedy of becoming an addict myself, it never occurred to me how much my actions and choices were hurting those who loved me. When mental health spirals out of control, it is just as dangerous as an addict. I was on a destructive path, and gradually, my friends and even family members started to fade away. Not only did they not know what I was going through, but they certainly didn't understand the choices I was making.

I thought I was in the clear by this time, but even with starting medicine and trialing the right fit for my prescription, I was still in a downward spiral that led to my rock bottom moment.

In a moment of a black hole-like depressive state, I once again considered and attempted to take my own life. It's difficult to explain how one can be in a marriage with a person you love but still be experiencing such loneliness from the rest of the world that there was just no light at the end of the tunnel in my mind and escaping was the only way out.

After intentionally taking too many prescription pills, the medicine haze started to kick in, but Brian found me and took me to the emergency room. It was here, and after hours of observation, that they determined that the only option was for me to check into a behavioral health hospital.

The next hour or two of my life is one of my most vivid memories from my twenties. Even though I don't desire to remember this moment in time, it is ingrained in my head. It's a constant reminder of what rock bottom looks and feels like. Of all the memories that are unclear to me, for some reason, this one may never go away.

The unit doors swing shut. They are clear, so I can see Brian walking away, down the hall. He's been escorted out by a woman in a coat, I assume a doctor, who reaches her arm against his back and taps the middle in between his shoulder blades as if she's comforting a friend she's known forever.

The nurse is holding my arm just above my elbow, not hard, but just enough that as I force my body against the door, her grip tightens, and I feel her nails just barely clench against my skin.

"Brian! Please just let me just talk to him! Brian!" I scream it, and I see his head just slightly turn towards me. I don't even see his full face, but as he rounds the corner, he waves his hand out from his side at me, just a little, and then he's gone.

My body instantly falls to the floor, and the nurse lets go. I can feel the cold all along my side that touches the tile. I'm wearing nothing but a thin gown and a pair of hospital socks. She lets me lay there for a minute. I'm shaking, tears just falling to the floor and into my hair which sticks to my face as I lay there curled up. I slowly go quiet, gasping for air as my screams fade into just the hyperventilation of sobs mixed with occasional breaths.

"Come on," she says calmly, "I'll show you your room." She kneels beside me and moves my hair out of my face. She reaches for my hand. I slowly grab it and pull myself up with her help.

I look up, and at least five girls are staring at me, all in gowns too; all of them look about my age, mid to early twenties, maybe some of them even as young as eighteen or so. I could tell by their stares that they had all been here too. This was part of it. They looked sad for me, but their stares told me they understood. They weren't judging me. They just knew. Nobody said anything as the nurse walked me past them and into a room just down the hall.

Five days I spent in this ward. Five days of feeling every ounce of shame in life a girl could fathom. Other than Brian and our families, nobody even knew I was there. I never even called into work. It was simply a disappearance. I think Brian called and gave some excuse for me at the time, but that was it. It was like I was finally swept off the face of the planet and thrown into this world that I never imagined would ever be mine.

I remember feeling so "above" the other girls there. I listened to their problems and stories as they talked in group therapy, and even though I sat beside them with problems of my own, I still held this mentality that I didn't belong.

About two days in, a nurse explained the process of how I could get out. I had to fully accept the terms of where I was. "You have to understand, Sara, that you are here for a reason, and we can't let you leave without proof that you have really made a difference and you are not going to end up back here," she explained.

I had been so cold towards everyone there, never opening up once about what was going on inside, even to those who would probably understand more than everyone. After listening to the nurse, I realized that I wasn't going home if I didn't open up.

So with the start of my third day, I shifted my mindset. I was no better than anyone here. This was not my choice to be here, and as much as I hated every moment in this unit, I realized that it was this or nothing. I had no other options. I needed to fix what brought me here, and more than going back to work—which weighed heavily on my mind—I needed to work on myself. It was literally the only thing left that mattered.

The morning of the third day, right after breakfast, we did a group therapy session where the doctor had us write out our dream life in five years. Everyone else around me was quietly writing, and I just stared at my blank sheet contemplating. What did I want? I was twenty-eight years old, and I had lost nearly every friend in my life—the ones remaining were starting to have kids. All I had left was one man, and I wasn't even sure he'd still be there when I got out. What I wanted was that same dream I wanted as a little girl.

My dream was no different than it had ever been. I wanted to be a mother; I wanted to live in a house in a suburb with my children and husband and dogs running around the house, loud and crazy as ever. I wanted to have a group of friends and neighbors and throw big family parties where the kids ran around for hours playing as the adults talked and laughed and played card games. I wanted to attend my kids' school plays and sporting events and cheer them on from the sidelines just like my parents did for me. That was my dream. That was my happy. All I could think about was how unobtainable that dream had become.

The doctor walked over, read a little blurb from my paper over my shoulder, and said, "I think this is a pretty great vision for you, and I see that journey for you too. Let's make it happen."

The day I left the hospital, Brian came in for a joint therapy session to talk with my doctor about my progress and plan moving forward. We talked about my vision and my dreams for our future. We sat in that room, both crying and broken, neither of us sure at all that any of it was possible as much as we both wanted the same things so badly for our future together.

I vowed to change, seek help and permanent treatment, and I knew that if I messed up again, that would be it. This was my last chance at the life I had always dreamed could be mine. There was no turning back, and there was no more room for error.

The next six months or so was a steady grind, one where I quietly re-entered the world. I was completely shattered, and I gently had to put back the pieces of my life, one by one. As broken as I was when we left that hospital, Brian never left my side. Just like my mom had done to my dad when I was a teenager, and as much as I didn't understand it then for what she did by staying with him, Brian did the same for me.

Less than a year after walking out of that hospital together, we found out we were expecting our first baby—our little boy and the biggest life-changing soul on the planet for me up until that point, Cameron. And just like that, in the blink of an eye, the world I once knew was no longer the same.

Just like I had written out on that paper in the hospital, this was truly the beginning of my journey towards a new happiness I had never experienced before in my life. My journey to becoming a mother changed me forever. Becoming a mother came with a million challenges of its own. I decided to stay home full-time with Cameron, and it was only a year later when we found out Chloe was on her way too.

To stay home full-time with my kids, I decided to turn my hobby into a full-time career. I opened a photography studio and business, which took off faster than I ever could have imagined. None of it came easily to me. As much as I thrived on motherhood, working on myself and my happiness was a full-time job in itself.

After a few years, our final baby, Livie, came along; our family was complete. Not long after she was born, I went back to work full-time again. I had been a stay-at-home mom, owned my own business, and was actively following my heart on what I felt like was my journey towards continued happiness.

I've learned that happiness is not a destination; it resides on a spectrum. I have the three most beautiful children whom, at one point in my journey, even up until that walk out of the hospital that day, I never thought possible. I am married to a person who accepts me for me and loves me despite my flaws. While I don't regret my past, sometimes I think about what my life would have been like had I addressed some of these issues way back before they all blew up in my face.

We are not immune to anything in this world, and we are certainly not promised happiness from anyone. I am happy today because I have worked and continue to work really, really hard at it. Maybe I've had to work harder than some, yes, but if you are going through something small or you are unhappy with certain things in your life, you owe it to yourself to work through it. I hit rock bottom more than once, and somehow, I was able to once again find my way after it all came crashing down on me.

And if you choose to avoid life's challenges or your problems, and keep pushing away that little voice in your head telling you that something just isn't right, then I assure you, it will catch up with you down the road. To this very day, I still take medication and have moments where I struggle just as everyone else does, but I have decided that my imperfect mental health, nor my past, will hold me back from my goals and dreams in life. I didn't just want to survive; I wanted to create the amazing life I had once dreamed of as a kid.

When I started to get better, I was still so ashamed of my past and thought I would be so different from my peers as an adult and a mom now. I thought that since I had these major tragedies in my life, I wasn't going to relate to anyone anymore. But when I started listening and meeting people in the same place in life as me, mid-20s, having kids, and so on, I realized how many people, even though they were leading very "normal" lives, were just really struggling daily. Even without anything significant happening, the struggle, as they say, was real.

Discord with spouses, struggling with infertility, dealing with a family member or someone with addiction, postpartum depression, eating disorders, general anxiety, parenting frustrations, anger issues, financial issues, marriage issues, or just not being satisfied with their career or day-to-day life affected nearly everyone I met. Everyone I knew was looking for a place to vent; everyone I knew was looking for ways to make themselves happier; everyone was looking for someone to relate to.

The term mental illness slowly started seeping into the language of the "normal" friends in my life, not just people who had dealt with traumatic experiences like I once thought. My tragedies started to not feel so unrelatable, and slowly, I started to feel like I was actually more normal than I ever knew. Whether you've been diagnosed with mental illness or not, I'm here to tell you that you deserve more, and you are actually way more normal than you may even realize.

There is a road to happy. It's there. It may not be a one-way street, it may wind and turn and go in circles, but it's there. You just have to keep going. Each of us deserves happiness, but it certainly won't be waiting for you to just fall upon when you finally receive that promotion or finally buy that big house or fancy car. You need to work for it every day, little by little and moment by moment, and if you do, happiness is there, and it's worth it.

How to Get the Most Out of This Book: "Using your Rules of the Road" Workbook

This book contains seven principles—your rules of the road...come on, you've gotta live by the theme here, okay? Each rule is its own chapter, where I discuss how I've personally struggled with it and then the techniques I use to cope with that struggle. To gain the best benefit from this book, read through it with a pen in hand. After you've read about my experience, reflect on how it resonates with you, then write down ideas and observations that arise and what you can do right now to make those changes.

The back of the book contains a **Rules of the Road Workbook** where you can write your answers and thoughts directly you read. You can also download a printable version or have a separate workbook mailed to you— head over to **www.saraglashagel.com** for your own separate copy of this workbook.

I highly recommend taking your time and being honest and vulnerable in this process by writing down your answers and thoughts as you go. Each of these activities was intentionally created to help you best work on yourself moving forward.

I promise that no matter what you are going through, making these changes will make a difference in your life if you stick to it. I have provided plenty of room for you to write your thoughts, and the best part about this is that you can come back weeks or months later and write down how you are doing, what you can do better, and what insights you've gained.

Like having a report card, keeping up with the journal prompts within this book will hopefully keep you focused throughout the year. I hope this book offers more than a "read it and forget it" method.

When you get to the workbook portion of each principle, be honest. Nobody else is reading this but you. Keep it in a place where even your spouse can't find it if you're concerned about sharing these feelings. If you can't write down honest answers for yourself, then it's going to be even harder to follow some of my suggestions, including being honest about your struggles with those who matter to you in life.

Health Disclaimer: I am not a therapist, and if you are experiencing something really traumatic—it may be current, or perhaps it is something from the past you still struggle with—I wholeheartedly believe in the benefits of counseling and medical advice. Whether you visit a psychiatrist or your primary caregiver, medical direction is crucial to dealing with any type of mental illness.

You might be thinking, "Oh, I don't need help because I just get anxious or overwhelmed," or "I am just going through a rough patch; I'll get through it." Though it may seem small, these topics are worth discussing with medical professionals and people trained to help you get through these challenges. As I said, I take medication and see a therapist. I do this because I know that even though I may be in a healthy place today, I may run into something bigger than I can manage to handle. I am not ashamed to admit that I take medicine. My brain is chemically imbalanced, and I know that. I know that the way to be my healthiest self is to take that medicine.

I also know that even while taking action on what I suggest in this book, I still need someone to talk to on occasion. I don't see the therapist nearly as often as I used to, but I still have regular appointments because I know that if I stop, I may start to fall into my old pitfalls, and things can quickly pile up without me even realizing it. Sometimes many avenues are required to get through a rough stage in life. If life is hitting you hard right now, please, seek help.

Also, read this book. Follow the suggestions and answer the questions. Be completely honest and transparent with yourself. It's not easy, but it will be worth the effort.

Stop Comparing
Comparison Is The Thief Of Joy

If you are anything like me, you've probably spent your fair share of endless hours scrolling through all of the different social media channels. When so many platforms are available, it's hard to avoid. When I was at some super-low points in my life, I couldn't even look at social media without crying.

I only saw people happier than me doing things that I didn't feel I would ever be able to do. After I was home from the hospital in my twenties, I remember logging onto social media for the first time, and I felt as if I couldn't relate to anyone. People I knew were going on vacation, having babies, leading fun-filled everyday lives. I was stuck at home, barely able to function and make it day-to-day.

I had points in my life when I chose to block certain friends from my social media account because seeing their content was just too painful. If you've ever gone through a breakup, you know what I'm saying.

Blocking friends from social media is more common than it seems. I don't know a single person who hasn't done this. So, if you are reading this and blocking seems insane to you, well, then, I guess you are just not as crazy as the rest of us—and more power to you if you've got the discipline not to block.

I remember a time right after I had come out of the hospital. I was focused on getting healthy, and I was doing all the right things to get myself in a good place again, yet I found myself completely obsessed with seeing what all of my friends were doing on social media. I realized that I had become wholly overwhelmed with jealously about their lives while telling myself I was not nearly as successful or having as much fun as they were. I had to actively shut off my social media for at least a month because my emotional attachment to their posts was literally driving me crazy.

As time went on, I had to make a decision that I had to stop thinking about them and instead make life happen for myself. I stopped checking their profiles and even unfollowed many of them for the time being. What was it doing to help me? These were friends and family members I loved and still cared for, and the constant reminder that they were still happy and leading these joyful lives wasn't working for me. I needed to focus on living my own life and getting myself happy.

And even now that I have kids and a family and things are going really well, for the most part, I am very intentional about not living my life through social media. If my family has done something fun, sure, I'll share it on occasion. However, I also have had to stop myself from posting something *just* so that others will see what I'm doing and like it.

I've realized experiences are far more enjoyable when I can just live in the moment and pay little attention to updating the world on what I'm doing.

In turn, I also check social media *way* less than I ever used to.

I love social media, don't get me wrong. I absolutely love that I can stay in touch with friends from college, see what my old coworkers are up to, follow my cousins across the country, and share my children and family's adventures with all of them, as well. But the biggest trap I'd fall into, especially if I were in a moment of depression, was looking at someone else on social media and feeling jealous.

So you think that the person you're jealous of has it all? Believe me, they don't. Social media is designed to make yourself look your best. Filters, selfies, and celebrity content drives our standards. It flames people's desire to fit in and keep up in a world where perfection is the standard. The worst time to step into this trap is when you are struggling with something; then, poof, up pops someone showing off their perfect life, completely struggle-free.

Everyone deals with life challenges. Everyone has a story; they're just not going to share it on social media. Consider looking at social media with the filter in your mind that it is a tool to highlight happy moments, not one that highlights the struggles. I can almost promise you that the neighbor down the street who posts perfect matching-clothed photos of her children in the ideal setting had to fight with at least one of those kids to wear that, and quite possibly, a bribe was involved. I know this because I am a photographer, and oh yeah, I'm often the person taking those perfect photos for families. Ironic, huh?

If you've never done a family photo shoot, let me break it down for you. Ninety percent of my clients, with or without kids, tell me before, after, or even during the photo shoot how stressful it was to get everything perfect. "Yeah," I tell them, "perfect is a pretty high standard. Maybe we should shoot for real instead." Finding the perfect outfits, doing hair and makeup, getting the kids all ready to go, convincing their spouse that this is even worth the money and time to do; all of that takes time and effort and creates even more anxiety than if you weren't going to do these photos in the first place.

But why do we do it? For many of us, it's because it's a way to show our family life to the world and say, "Look, we've got it all together!" But I'm telling you—okay, maybe begging you—as valuable as it is to have family photos as displayable memories and reminders of how much we love these people, please, please don't look at other people's photos with one ounce of jealousy. I am here to tell you that, in truth, getting those seemingly perfect photos caused as much anxiety for them as they do for you. And guess what, they also have looked at another person's photos and thought, "Gosh, I want our family to look like that, or dress like that, or be as perfect as them."

Let me be clear; I, too, am guilty of these things. I run a photography business off the premise that having family photos with correctly coordinating outfits is essential and valuable. Yes, I believe it, but I am always real with people when they come to me for photos. I give an outfit guide, and I offer tips on setting up for a successful shoot, but I also tell my clients that these photos capture a time in your life. They don't capture perfection.

Do you know how many moms with uncooperative children I have had to talk off the ledge because a child wasn't smiling or wasn't behaving? So so many. "Listen, this is who your one-year-old is right now. He may not be sitting and smiling for photos, but I am going to capture him playing with you or even some tears, and I promise you will look back on these pictures in a few decades and remember that he was a little stinker, and that is okay!"

I really love doing family photos for my family every year. If I'm honest, we probably have photo sessions more than once a year. However, I've changed my mindset from "I can't wait for people to see how we look on social media" to "I am so excited to have these photos to hang and remember how we all looked and changed so much every year as the kids get older." Do I still share on social media? Yes. But social media is no longer my why. Do I think you should stop sharing your photos? No, but give some thought to *your* why.

It's okay to share your family and what makes you happy, but it's also pretty freeing to caption some of your photos with the reality of the shoot. Because the truth of my family's shoot is that, first of all, my husband does *not* find the same joy out of taking photos as I do. He is pretty much always grumpy when we do family photos. He's getting better, and he does it solely because he knows it's important to me, so he sucks it up.

My kids usually do well during photos because they, like my husband, have learned that mommy really cares about these pictures. Not to mention the fact that, oh yeah, I've also often bribed them with something to do it. When someone comments on my photo that we're the perfect family, I just cannot help but laugh. Ha! We are so far from perfect. We argue and scream; we say things we don't mean. It's pretty hard to see all of that in a photo. So my advice is post away with those perfect photos, my friends, but do it with a little hint of honesty and realism in your caption.

You'd be surprised how many more people will relate to a real post than a "look how perfect we are" post.

Aside from the photos on social media depicting a perfect life, there is also this lovely little feature we all now get to experience called filters. Ahh, yes, filters. I use them. They make me feel better when I'm not wearing makeup or when I have bags under my eyes. There's something kind of nice about a smoothing feature when you're over thirty-five, just saying. Filters are fun, but they can also be dangerous if you're not careful. Ever looked at a celebrity or influencer's photos online and immediately thought, "How do they manage to look like that?" Well, I have! The answer—if it isn't a professional hair and makeup team, professional beauty treatments, professional editing, or surgeries—is filters.

Filters provide just another way for people to feel better about themselves and ensure other people see them in a better light. These days it's difficult to notice the difference between a photoshopped photo and a regular photo. Some apps morph your body, some can change your hair or eye color, and all of them are getting so good that you literally cannot tell the difference sometimes. Don't let these fool you.

Yes, it's totally fine to post a picture with a good angle or take twenty pictures and only post one. I've done it myself. It's valid to want to take a good photo or touch something up, so it looks a bit better. But you need to know that quite honestly, nobody else is out there worried about the angle of your photo any more than you are. And what you see on these celebrities or influencers all over social media is often a very deliberate edit or the product of a hundred photos to get one perfect one, just for the sake of making themselves look perfect.

I don't knock anyone for trying to make themselves feel better for using something like this. I am the queen of checking a photo of myself taken by someone else before I let them post it. How many times do you take a photo, and someone says, "Let me see!" Yeah, almost all the time, right? That's just this generation. Even kids as young as three and four during photo shoots ask to see the back of my camera when I take their picture.

This is our society, and it's okay, but you can't let those photos be your source of joy. You can't look at someone else's images and allow them to take away your happiness. When a car passes you on the road, you don't need to catch up to that car, and you don't need to swerve around it. Just stay in your lane. Worry about your own driving, your own life, and your own happiness.

When it comes to comparing yourself to others, keep in mind that as great as some else's world may look, there is always more to a story than you know. Everyone is dealing with something, and you never honestly know what is behind the closed doors of someone's house. Rather than wasting your time focusing on someone else's accomplishments and life milestones, put that energy into your own life and happiness.

And if you happen to catch yourself taking a photo solely to post it online, I recommend you take a moment and question your motives. Is this a photo you would take if social media didn't exist? Are you taking this photo because you want to remember this moment forever and save it, or is it something you are looking to post with the sole hope that you will end up getting likes and comments?

If it's the latter, try holding off. Take the picture, and *don't* post it. Have a get-together with friends and don't take a picture every time. Allow yourself to just enjoy some of those moments in life without the constant need to share for recognition's sake. Focus on the actual joy of the moment over the joy of receiving likes. In the long run, that joy is what matters the most anyway.

Complete "Rules of the Road"
Rule #1 Activity on **page 97**

Be Honest With Yourself

For many of the ten to fifteen years when I struggled most with mental illness, I avoided addressing my issues. It was easier to contemplate and talk about my parents' issues, but I was only hurting myself by not addressing my problems. I was quick to blame everyone else around me and spent very little time reflecting on what it was I needed to fix.

When you have a loved one dealing with something like addiction or you've experienced other traumas in your life—such as domestic violence or any other type of abuse—it becomes easy to blame the other person. He or she becomes the culprit and origin of all of your problems. Yes, your current challenges likely stem from those experiences. However, blaming your poor actions and choices on that experience is not being honest with yourself.

Part of my issue was that I didn't even realize I had a problem. I knew my dad had a problem with drugs. Yet, I spent way too many years causing my own problems that had nothing to do with him. He messed up, so I allowed myself to live with the excuse that "I'm like this because of him." But, had someone stopped me and told me that my behavior and choices were unacceptable, or had I been in tune with this myself, I could have saved myself from a lot of unnecessary stress and further trauma.

A couple of years back, I was in a counseling session. We discussed what was going on in my life and how I was dealing with current stress. She asked me a question that I don't know I've ever been asked before in my life, "Are you truly happy?"

I didn't have an answer right away. Yes, I had recovered from all of the trauma of my teens and early twenties for the most part. My parents were back together and living twenty minutes away. My kids were healthy and happy. My marriage with Brian was great. But that didn't answer the question.

All of those things made me happy, sure, but was I really, truly happy? I had never really thought about it. I had never sat down and had an honest conversation with myself about how to *intentionally* achieve true happiness. It's pretty easy to sit back in life and let things happen and just go along for the ride. I had kind of come to that point in my life where things were good, life was simple, but I was coasting.

She gave me a homework assignment. I was to go home and write down the things that made me happy, and then for each one, I needed to write my why.

I realized that, even though I was generally feeling good, coasting, and moving along from day to day without much "unhappiness," so to speak, I also wasn't focused on being honest with myself about the little everyday things that caused frustration to build up. I now know that I need occasional time alone, away from my family, to recharge from the routine of every day.

I regularly spend time with different groups of people, all outside of my family, and I have grown to so much appreciate these nights away. I am constantly telling Brian to do the same when I can tell he is getting stressed. There's something about being a parent and having the same daily routine and stressors that cause us to need a solid break now and then.

It sounds so cliche in the mom world, but a good old-fashioned girls' night is so good for me. Without a doubt, I'm a better wife and mother for the rest of the week after I come home. Having an outlet like this is a form of self-care. My husband even admits he loves and values the time he has when he's out to dinner and just hanging out with a bunch of friends or when he goes to a buddy's house to watch a basketball game at night.

Time alone is also super important, no matter what type of relationship or living situation you are in. I realized I needed this because I'd reach a boiling point with stupid little things and explode on everyone. Noticing these triggers, identifying them, and then being able to express a solid statement to everyone in my household that, "Mommy loves you all, but I need a minute!" was a healthy step forward for me.

But how do you even recognize that there is an issue with your happiness? How do you determine things that take away from your contentment? I think we often get used to our life as it is, even if the norm is being anxious, frustrated, sad, or angry. Think about your relationship with your significant other. Consider how easy it is to fall into a pattern of arguing over chores, money, or taking care of the kids.

One of the biggest arguments between Brian and me—and one I have heard echoed often in the mom community—is the controversy over where each spouse brings value to the relationship. For example, what's the value in doing the dishes, taking the kids to school, working, staying at home, making meals? We have gone through periods where we pick on each other about these little things, and the result is that happiness in both our lives diminishes.

Being honest with yourself, especially when you are in a relationship, requires reflecting on your behavior and how you react to and treat the other person. My old pattern used to be that no matter what went wrong, it was just easiest—and almost came naturally— that I blamed Brian for pretty much everything. I tended to play the victim rather than take ownership over my role in an argument. Even about petty stuff, I would just place the blame and point the finger back at him.

He didn't help with the dishes; he didn't help with the laundry; he didn't do this or that for the kids. I easily pointed the finger at him all the time. But at some point, I realized that I needed to be honest with myself and take some serious ownership over the fact that, as a team in this relationship, there are just truly things that fall on my plate.

When Brian is home, he does help with a ton of stuff. Does he do everything I do? No, not even close. But he also does about a hundred things around the house that I don't do, so rather than immediately giving him attitude because I feel overwhelmed, I've learned to stop and switch my mindset.

Once I did this and started looking at how mean I was when we'd argue, all of a sudden, it occurred to me that I would never want him to talk to me the way that I talked to him. I would allow myself to get overwhelmed with laundry or dishes or the kids, and as much as he was helping, I was letting my lack of time management get in the way, and in turn, I took out all of that stress and frustration directly on him.

Now when I am overwhelmed, I've learned to take ownership over the situation and ask myself how can I better manage my time? What chores can I let slide for a bit so I don't feel so overwhelmed? Do I spend too much time scrolling apps and watching Netflix when I probably could be at least multi-tasking with those things at the very least?

Two things that I dislike the most in the world are laundry and dishes, so I've started to listening to podcasts while I do both. It may sound so silly, but for me, listening to podcasts or even books on tape are two things that I love to do but never seem to have time for. So now when I am doing those stupid, meaningless, but necessary tasks—that, guess what, I have to do because otherwise, they're not getting done—I now put in my head-phones, and *bam*, I'm officially now doing something I love, and I'm not overwhelmed while I'm doing the stuff I don't like.

I've realized that with a full-time job and three kids, grocery shopping was extremely stressful. I literally ran out of time in my days and the last thing I wanted to do at the end of the day was go shop. So I was honest with myself, swallowed my pride in being the do-it-all mom, and guess what I've discovered that is the all-time greatest thing on the planet? Grocery delivery service.

Now is this for everyone? Nope, not at all. Some people have time to do this in their day, or maybe they are just better at making time in their day for it. But for me, this extra two hours a week was causing me way too much stress, so after fixing the problem, I've eliminated that stressor in my life, and now, my favorite thing ever is opening my door to twenty bags of groceries for the week for my family, and it's the greatest breath of fresh air ever.

Most likely, if you can be completely honest with yourself, take some ownership over a situation that is causing stress, and identify your triggers, you will almost always find a solution that isn't about the other person. It's about yourself. And guess what, you can probably easily fix it too.

If you find yourself stressed, frustrated, angry, yelling, or sad most of your days, I am here to tell you that is not how it should be. If this is the case, you need to stop and have an honest conversation with yourself and do some serious soul-searching about what is causing this and how you can change it.

Understanding these triggers is the simple fact that it's really easy to pretend you are happy and to put on a front. However, if you aren't truly honest with yourself—identifying your weaknesses and the areas where you can keep growing—then you're doing yourself a pretty strong disservice. Also, it's just as important to know what your strengths are as it is to know your weaknesses.

When you recognize your strengths, you have endless possibilities in this world, regardless of your life's struggles. I have always known, without a shadow of a doubt, that I am an excellent people person. I'm an extrovert and love talking to just about anyone I meet. I love learning about people and helping them. I eventually discovered that I have excellent emotional intelligence, and with that came a ton of opportunities.

Even with my past challenges, I am naturally able to understand other people's feelings and emotions. Knowing this about myself allowed me to look for positions where I could capitalize on this and thrive in careers that tie specifically to these strengths. If I hadn't taken the time to explore and understand what I'm inherently good at, I'd likely be in a job where I'm bored or just barely making it through the day with zero motivation, but instead, my work is actually doing exactly what I am good at and love, which makes it effortless and enjoyable.

I've spoken to many people who are unsatisfied with their jobs, and I've heard this same complaint time and time again that they are just wasting their days at this dead-end career where they are bored or unhappy. This may sound too easy of a solution, but I'm going to make this very straightforward for you here. If you are one of the dissatisfied people, I have two questions for you: 1. What are you good at, and are you currently doing this at your job? 2. What do you love, and are you currently doing this at your job? If your answers to these questions do not describe your current job, then my next question is simply, "Why are you still there?"

Now, does this mean that I think everyone can be doing their dream job? No, I understand that the reality, in many cases, that just is not possible. I get it. We live in a crazy, unstable economy where job security doesn't come easily. People often must do a job that they don't love because they need to provide for their families.

If this is you, please know that I see you and I hear you, and I believe that if this is you I am speaking to, then I know you are doing the best you can for your family and have my utmost respect. I commend you for working to support whoever it is that you are supporting. But I also will say this, while you are at that job, keep searching. Keep your dreams alive. Be honest with yourself and your goals in life and keep them alive.

I can honestly say that I have spent years in positions where I was not doing what I loved and was not using my strengths to the fullest of my abilities, but I didn't stop working. I knew I had bigger goals and bigger dreams, and I kept working toward them. My bosses today will even tell you, they know, even right now, in the job that I love, I have bigger dreams to accomplish. I've made it known that I'm not done, and I'm going to keep working towards something bigger. I don't even know what that is entirely, but I know that I'm just not done.

But I can also confidently say that I am happy with my job day in and day out. I love what I do. I love the people I work with. I love going to work. Even within the business I own, I am truly just doing things that make me happy. That's the goal. And I got there with continual honest conversations with myself and what I truly desired in life.

Complete "Rules of the Road" Rule #2 Activity on **page 99**

Be Honest With Those You Love

I spent so much of my life just hiding the truth from everyone that the lies themselves became more hurtful than some of my actual actions. Mental health is not something anyone ever talked about in my childhood. Even in high school, we had home economics, tech classes, sex education, but never once did a teacher address mental illness and what it looks like. I am grateful that many schools now teach in a style that uses social-emotional learning, a method that teaches kids at a young age to recognize feelings and emotions in themselves and others.

These days, at the high school level, teachers have been trained to recognize students who need guidance with mental health and have specific protocols to follow. Even with these standards in place at so many schools, there is still a whole generation of adults who have never once discussed mental health in an educational setting and are conditioned to hide their struggles from society.

When I gradually started talking about my anxiety and other issues, the floodgates of those who were listening just opened up. I began to learn how many of my friends, coworkers, and fellow moms were struggling. I may not have told my full story to everyone, but it became essential for me, anytime I found a person in my life who I fully trusted and was in my inner circle, to be fully transparent with them about what I had been through.

A part of knowing who I am as a friend is understanding where I've come from in my life. I've had many hard conversations. Every time, I was embarrassed a little, ashamed a little. Yet, every time I opened up to someone, it was freeing, and it felt as if a major weight lifted off my shoulders. The more I was honest with someone, the closer we became as friends. I now define a friend differently than I once did in my life. I now value my friendships more than I ever did before. In the past, I was always a fun friend, but I wasn't exactly an honest friend. The relationships in my youth were not as strong because of my false front.

This does not mean I tell everyone I meet my story—well, until now, I suppose—but with each person I talk to about challenging topics like this, it gets easier and easier. I think and hope that we may be getting to the point in society where talking openly about mental illness is finally becoming acceptable. It's just time. It's time.

One of the benefits of discussing your challenges with those around you is that you will quickly develop a network of others dealing with similar issues. Even more than that, by being brave and opening the conversation, you open the door for someone else to now feel comfortable talking about something they may have been holding in for a long time.

A few years back, I mentioned in a group that I struggled with an eating disorder. Not more than a few minutes passed before at least four other women opened up and admitted that they also had struggled with eating issues at one time in their life. I was shocked. Based solely on stereotypes, these were women that I would have never pegged as having eating disorders. Suddenly, it became almost a group therapy session about how everyone had dealt with it and overcome it. A few of the women even admitted that they still struggled to this day.

After a long conversation, at least one of those women decided it was time she got back into some sort of therapy or treatment because her eating disorder had gotten pretty bad in recent years. But until this group, she hadn't ever told anyone. My wavering but brave step of admitting my own issue helped someone else figure out they probably needed treatment.

Allowing the fear of being judged or shamed is the easy path. It's easy to convince yourself that people won't love you or accept you if you're honest. If we go on with life allowing ourselves to stay silent due to fear or shame, we miss out on so many opportunities, relationships, and successes. We cut ourselves off because we perceive our challenges are too scary to talk about. We choose not to speak, and we miss out on joy.

It was not that long ago that I interviewed for the position in my current company. The interviewer, who became my boss, asked what I thought would be the most challenging part of the position. He asked what I usually struggled with most. One of the biggest struggles in my past positions is that sometimes job stress gets to be too much for me; I often break under pressure. That answer was pretty scary to admit to a future employer, especially when you're trying to convince him to hire you for a position that comes with a lot of stress. I had a moment in my mind where I quickly debated coming up with some sort of a fake answer, one that wouldn't scare him away. Then, from a *new* habit I'd recently adopted, I told the truth.

I told him that I had previously come to a breaking point with the stress of a job. I may have even used the word anxiety—scary, I know! Much to my surprise, he almost immediately agreed that he struggled with stress and anxiety in the past, as well. Mid-interview, he even began to open up a little about some of the specifics of anxiety he had dealt with in the past. Rather than scare him away, I had immediately become relatable and real.

He didn't just view me as someone who had occasionally gotten in over her head in the past. Instead, he saw me as a person who was truly honest with my answer. As far as getting the job, he even mentioned to me later on in the process how relatable I had been. He said he appreciated the raw honesty in my answers. He even admitted that they specifically look for people who can be honest, even if it's not the answer that other employers may view as the *right* answer. They would rather hire someone vulnerable, who knows their flaws, can identify them, and learn from them to get better.

Wouldn't you rather have someone working for you who can learn from their mistakes rather than someone stuck in their ways? Sometimes being vulnerable and real is one hundred times better than someone perfect and without flaws.

Even now, in this current position, most of my team knows that I am a workaholic. I put way more pressure on myself than any of them will ever put on me, and I am a perfectionist and am constantly fighting to outperform myself from the month before. In a past life, I can see where sharing information about my flaws with people would almost be frowned upon.

How could I tell them my weaknesses? How could I share that I am going to stress myself out in this job? Maybe they would fire me because they would think I couldn't handle it. But instead, it's exactly the opposite. I often have members of my team who will remind me that I need to give myself a break or go easier on myself.

It is through my ability to be honest with them that I can, in turn, receive help with some of these areas when I get too stressed or anxious about something going on at work. Not only that, but this complete honesty is mutual, and so it's just very common that someone else is just as comfortable sharing their own weaknesses with me in that same place of vulnerability.

Maybe you're the type of person who doesn't necessarily have something you're embarrassed to admit or ashamed of, but perhaps you've held back because you don't think anyone will care, or you fear people will reject you or look down on you. I have a good friend who struggles with a really hard life experience. Her daughter has some pretty severe special needs, and even though she is one of my closest friends, she often used to say things like, "You won't understand," or "I feel so lonely because I have nobody to talk to about it."

This friend and I talk all the time, and I cannot tell you how many times I used to reply, "Who cares? Just talk to me. I don't have to understand, but I want to listen." And it's true, I don't always understand and certainly don't always know the right thing to say in the moment, but I can empathize with the pain she's facing. By allowing her to talk, all I have to do is listen; and with just that, I'm helping.

After a while of inviting her to let down her guard and open up to me, she finally did and now often confides in me things that I don't always have advice for. She knows that, but she also trusts that I will be there for her regardless without judgment. In fact, I rarely actually have advice to give her. I've never had a child with special needs, and I don't know the daily trauma that they face in their family, but I know how to listen. I know how to say, "I'm sorry you're dealing with that," when she's struggling.

Because I choose to listen, she continues to call and talk about stuff. Even though I don't always have the right words to say, she simply wants to be heard. She knows that I'm part of her tribe, and I may not be a fellow special needs mom, but she knows that when she's struggling, I'm a safe space and an ally. That's all people need is a safe space and an ally. You don't need to find someone who has gone through exactly your same journey.

Sometimes it feels difficult, but if you look, you can find an ally—someone who will listen, refrain from judgment, offer advice only when asked. Sometimes being heard is what people are looking for. When I'm struggling, and I choose to talk to people, I often say, "I don't even need you to respond. I just need to talk." Everyone needs an ally, and even more importantly, everyone needs to learn how to be an ally.

When someone comes to you for advice, you don't always need an answer. Sometimes answering makes it harder on the relationship. Take my friend with the daughter with special needs, for example. There were so many times years ago when she would talk and cry about what was going on, and I found myself continuing to tell her that she needed to go into therapy because I thought this situation was just too much for her to handle on her own. I said it out of love and because of my own personal experiences. I must've said it ten times. Eventually, I realized, maybe that's not the advice she needed. What service am I giving her by telling her something repeatedly with no result?

So I stopped telling her the same thing over and over. That's not what she needed to hear. It wasn't helping her, and if I would have continued to say it, all that does is put a wedge between us, which isn't helpful either. Being an ally for her didn't mean giving advice. In fact, if you listen, people often don't spill their problems and follow it up with, "What do I do?"

Therapy wasn't what she needed at the time. Many times, people just need to vent. They need to express their emotions, get it out, and move on. Unless you hear a "What do I do?" question, just listen. Empathize. Be present. You don't have to solve their problems. Just be an ally.

Complete "Rules of the Road"
Rule #3 Activity on **page 103**

Find What Fulfills You And Do More Of It

This one almost seems too obvious. I think we often forget to do what we love in life. What are you passionate about? What makes you *want* to get up in the morning? Are you doing it? It's easy to get in a rut without even realizing you're in one. Wake up, make breakfast, make lunches for kids, drive kids to school, go to work, grocery shop, get home, make dinner, get kids to bed, pass out on the couch. This, or some version of it, is a typical day for so many people.

Even if this is your routine, you likely have at least twelve hours in a day to do things you love—things that fill you up in life. But are you making the time for it? I realized that every now and then in life, I am so busy or so focused on the mundane, the routine, and the to-do's that I don't even have a minute for myself. Maybe it's only a few minutes here or there, but if you don't take the time to capitalize on this, then you are wasting some of the biggest opportunities to achieve happiness.

How do you go about adding those things into your life? First things first, examine your morning routine. This one was hard for me; I'll be the first to admit it. I am just *not* a morning person, and when people talked about waking up early to do something extra, I never saw that anything had greater value than sleep. But once I started getting up earlier, adding things I enjoyed in these morning times and got into a new routine, I can honestly say I will never go back.

We are so quick to just jump into the hustle of life—especially anyone with kids—time alone feels so hard to achieve. Trust me, I am not saying this is easy. It is anything but easy when you have children. Parents, if you are listening, this is my biggest piece of advice if you need time alone: *set your alarm to ring before your kids get up.* I repeat, set your alarm before your kids. Ensure you have quiet time for yourself, even if it's just thirty minutes. I've learned that the thirty minutes of alone time compared to the thirty minutes of sleep adds so much value to my day.

As parents, we are programmed to do everything for our children and put their needs before our own. Often it is incredibly difficult to prioritize yourself. Once I started with my mornings alone, it became one of my favorite times of the day because it was truly one of the only chunks of time all week where I just get to have some peace and quiet.

What you do with this time is up to you, and I think before just setting your alarm and waking up, you need to have a plan. Do you want to use your time to read, work out, meditate, write? There is no exact recipe for what you do with your time, but what I've found is that it's easy to get sucked into social media or turn on the news. Before you know it, the time is gone. So, regardless of what you decide to do with your time, be intentional with your use of it. Spend it doing things that you genuinely feel will benefit you the most. This is your time. What do you want to do with it?

I spend most of my mornings reading or writing because that's just what fulfills me and works for me. Pretty soon, thirty minutes was not enough, so I quickly decided I needed a full hour to myself. That was enough time to get my coffee and have plenty of time completely alone before anyone else in my house made a noise. Let me be clear here—*coffee fulfills me!*

I'm not saying you need to read or write in your spare time or even that you need to wake up early. But whether it's taking a break from your work during the day, going to the gym, going out to coffee with friends, meditating, staying up late when it's quiet, and everyone else is in bed, whatever it may look like for you, carving out time alone is so important, especially if you have children.

If you are not actively seeking out these little bits of self-fulfillment, then it is just way too easy to get back into that rut and those old habits of putting everyone else in your life first, and somehow, you fall to the end of the line again.

If you are intentional about this time, I promise you that you will see a significant difference. One of the reasons I increased my morning time from thirty to sixty minutes is that I added the use of affirmations to my regular reading. When I first learned about affirmations, I will readily admit that I scoffed. To me, the idea of saying something over and over just didn't work for me.

It worked for other people, and I was okay with that, but I didn't love the idea. That was until I learned about the concept of intention statements and ongoing goal setting as opposed to New Year's resolutions. Let me just tell you what happened in two words—*life-changing.*

I've always been a person who looked to quotes or looked to others for inspiration. Even when I was young, I loved the idea of quotes. I would write in my journal as a kid all sorts of quotes that inspired me to keep going; my house is full of those cheesy signboards everywhere you look, but all of that is there for a reason for me. I am not naturally optimistic.

I have always needed to put in the effort to become a positive person. When I learned about intention statements, it became a way for me to have those reminders—like a quote or a sign. However, these came in the form of a written reminder that I could look at every day. I started using it as fuel. When you create an intention statement or word, start by thinking about and writing down everything you want to work on or focus on.

My first ever intention word was simple, just two words: *self-love*. Once upon a time (okay, I still struggle with this), one of the hardest things for me was to stop using negative self-talk. Everyone around me saw the happy-go-lucky girl, the funny and sarcastic girl, the entrepreneur working so hard for her goals. But deep down inside, I was really cruel to myself. I'd look in the mirror and tear myself down about everything—the way I looked, the pounds on the scale, the amount of money I made. You name it, and I have insulted myself about it. So in January of 2020, before that global pandemic hit us, I wrote down *self-love* in a notebook, on my phone, next to my bed stand, and everywhere else I could think of.

I wrote it down in multiple places because I needed that constant reminder. I don't have it tattooed on me, but trust me, I thought about it. How could I preach to my daughters how beautiful they are and raise them with confidence when I didn't even have it myself. I worked on this concept all

year. I bought a simple journal, and when I woke in the morning, I'd immediately write down how I could love myself.

I became great at loving my kids when they were born. Why was it so much
harder to love me? Having the intention statement of self-love was the first
time I made it a focal point for me. No matter how hard I avoided it, I found
myself reminded day in and day out just to love myself. The more I learned
to do that, the better wife and mother I gradually started to become.

Brian will be the first to tell you that I still need to work on this. It doesn't
come naturally to me, and even with the year of it being my intention
statement, it is still something that I have to work on all the time. I probably always will, and that's okay, but I've made some serious progress. I'm
learning to look in the mirror and not just see imperfections, but instead
see a body that created three beautiful children.

I'm learning to stop looking at wrinkles and be mad that they're there, but
instead be grateful that I'm growing old with someone I love. I'm thankful
to watch our kids grow up and that I get to watch them start to live inde-
pendent lives as they develop their own personalities. I'm learning that the
more I love myself, the nicer I am to my husband and my children. The
more I love myself, I become a better friend because I stop focusing on my
issues and listen to and help others when they need it.

This intention statement of self-love also helped me understand that loving
myself means accepting that I owe it to myself to be selfish sometimes—
that putting myself first isn't selfish but necessary. Pedicures or massages
aren't just guilt-inducing selfish time-sucks. Instead, they are acts of self-
care and self-love that fulfill me and make me happy. I deserve those things

just as much as my kids deserve my time and attention. By taking care of myself in these ways, I return refreshed and able to genuinely love them better than I could if I wore myself down. Even events or trips with your friends, away from your significant other or family, is a truly valuable form of self-love and self-care. These are times to recharge your body and mind and should not be overlooked in a relationship.

And even though I've had intention words that I've focused on for months or weeks or even years at a time, I cannot tell you the number of constant reminders I still need. I have not perfected any of this. I am constantly trying to get better at this part in particular.

One of my best friends often reminds me of this. She knows that I have been working on self-love, well, ever since I've known her, and I think it's at least once a week that she will remind me of this when I am off and say something just mean about myself.

So not only do I have these intentions for myself, but those who are closest to me also know some of these areas where I am working on. Knowing that they know helps me stay humble and on track about these goals and these intentions. And I do the same for my friends. I am the queen of reminding my closest friends about something when I see them slip up on something they are personally working on in life. I don't ever remind them to rub it in; instead, as their friend, if I know they are working on something, why wouldn't I help them out? Isn't that what being a good friend is all about?

We are human and need reminders. Some of my favorite conversations with my friends are when we talk about the things that fulfill us or even what we're trying to work on in life. We hold each other accountable, and we are honest with each other out of love. When I slip up, I want my friends to call me out, and when they slip up, you better believe I will remind them of some of their greater goals.

There was an evening about a year ago when a group of neighbors and I were sitting around a campfire in our neighborhood talking. The topic of success came up, and one of my neighbors said something I've heard many times from people; "I will just be happy when..." I've heard this far too often from people, and I am just as guilty of saying this myself.

At those times when you're struggling and wanting something else to happen, it's easy to ignore living in the moment and finding the happiness where you're at. You instead put it off, basing it off of this perceived future success or milestone that you'll once hit. *I'll be happy when the baby is born. I'll be happy when I have this amount in my bank account. I'll be happy when I get a new job. I'll be happy when I get a boyfriend.* The list goes on and on, and I've done it a hundred times, and I know you have to, don't lie. But what about now? Being successful or making it to that one milestone isn't going to all of a sudden magically change the way you think.

If you are waiting for some magical life-milestone-fairy to come down and wave her magic wand, you should stop waiting now. I can assure you that if you make the conscious effort to *be* happy with what you have now, not only will you still make it to those successes, but you will actually achieve greater success in your life than if you sat around waiting.

Success does not lead to happiness. It is, in fact, quite the opposite. The more you open yourself up, feel fulfilled, and find joy in your current life, the easier you will find the doors of success opening up to you for your future.

In 2020, during the COVID-19 pandemic, I found myself wallowing in moments of boredom at home, wishing for the time when "we could all go back to normal." In the early months of our lockdown, as we were trapped inside during the bitter cold winter with an infant, a preschooler, and a kindergartener, I found myself sulking and feeling sorry for myself.

In the first few weeks, rather than really appreciating the time at home, I let opportunities for special moments pass me by. As time went on and reality set in, Brian and I talked about how we needed to change our attitudes.

We were the ones setting the example for our kids in this unforeseen situation, so it was our responsibility to show them how valuable the time at home was, rather than just wishing the clock would jump ahead. So we danced in our kitchen—an existing tradition in our home—played board games, built Lego cities, watched family movies, read books, and genuinely enjoyed our time together.

My husband, who typically coached spring sports, took on the role of the t-ball coach for my son. This opportunity, because of his full-time sports coaching schedule in addition to his teaching job, may never come again in our lives, to be quite honest. That is just the reality of his job and time commitments. But the memories of the two of them on the field together will always be a beautiful picture in my mind when I think back to the pandemic. We realized that this tragedy actually opened up some doors for our family. We turned something awful into a once-in-a-lifetime opportunity.

I know this pandemic was difficult for everyone. While some were more affected than others, especially due to reduced income or the loss of loved ones, it is rare chances like these when you get to take a lemon of a situation and turn it into lemonade. That is how you live truly fulfilled. You choose to see the good. You make the conscious effort of putting happiness and fulfillment in the forefront of your mind, and then you do the work to get there.

Success will not bring you happiness. On the contrary, happiness can absolutely bring you success.

If you are actively looking for success in your life, change your mindset. Focus on the things or people that you wrote above; focus on that feeling they bring you, and you will find success. I promise.

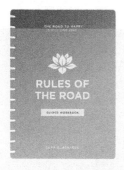

Complete "Rules of the Road"
Rule #4 Activity on **page 105**

Surround Yourself With People Who Make You Better

Life Coach Tony Gaskins once said, "Evaluate the people in your life; then promote, demote, or terminate. You are the CEO of your life." I read that quote, and at first, it sounds harsh. Terminate people from your life? But if you think about how many people have come and gone through the stages of your life by the time you are an adult, it doesn't feel all that terrible.

I think about when I was in high school. I remember the last night of summer before the first few of my friends left for college. I remember standing with my six best friends at the time, in the middle of a street. I couldn't tell you why we were in the middle of the street, but that's where we were. We stood in a circle, arms all wrapped around each other, crying. Crying because we knew, as young as we were, life would never be the same.

I remember the feeling that they were the only friends I would ever have, and I remember thinking that I would never be the same person I was at that moment without any of them at college. When you're in high school, oftentimes, your friends are your identity. Maybe more than any other time in your life, your friends represent everything about you.

For me, they were all I had to hold onto. The thought of terminating any of them intentionally from my life was just unheard of at the time.

I think about that group of us, now all in our mid-thirties, and nearly daily, I talk to *only one* of them. One. I once clung to these friends, and somehow almost all of them are no longer in my life. Of course, I see them on Facebook, and we comment on each other's photos here and there. But life happens, and people change. Your friends, as you become an adult, are just simply not all permanent fixtures in your life. People come and go in stages, but it is up to you to foster the relationships of those who make you better.

I want to speak about my one friend that I still talk with regularly. Our friendship has been through the wringer. We've been faced with as many challenges as any friendship could. In fact, when we were about twenty-five years old, she chose to cut me out of her life. The choices I was making did not fit her character at the time, and she could no longer be supportive of me and these choices. But life is funny, and as I said, you are in charge of who you surround yourself with—about four years ago, I reached out to her.

I apologized for everything that had happened in our friendship. For the first time, I explained how my choices arose from mental health issues. Even though we had a seven-year gap in our relationship, we are once again friends. I decided that, for me as an adult, she added value to my life. She challenged me. She inspired me. Even though years earlier she felt my choices didn't reflect her values, she was probably one of the strongest positive influences I ever had amidst the crazy that I was facing personally.

I've been through so many stages of friends in my life, and as I got older, I have learned the value of surrounding myself with people who are a positive influence. I don't owe anyone my friendship, and in return, nobody else owes me theirs. I've learned to be more selective than I once was in my teenage years. I've always been extraordinarily outgoing and easy to get along with. In fact, one of my current closest friends often tells me that I could be friends with anyone. She likes to say I "can talk to a wall" if I wanted. It's just in my nature. But I've learned to differentiate between being friendly with everyone and defining everyone as a friend.

My closest friends lift me up. They understand me at my best and my worst. They are people who don't judge me and can speak openly and honestly with me about anything. And my closest friends know exactly who they are, and that is because I think it is essential to let those who you love know their value in your life. When I find someone important to me, I let them know. Not because I need the affirmations in return, but because I want them to know how much I appreciate them, and on the days when I'm too busy to send a text or when weeks go by since I've seen them in person, they know how valuable they are to me because I've told them. There are no questions.

When you can find someone in your life, a friend you can speak honestly with, and they can be completely candid and honest in return, you need to take the time to realize and appreciate how insanely special that is. It is one thing if you can find a life partner who loves, challenges, and inspires you daily, but if you can find a friend who does the same, you need to stop and thank your lucky stars because it's not easy to find, and it certainly isn't easy to keep.

The relationships with our friends can be just as valuable as a relationship with a spouse. When you find a good friend, a person who makes you a better person, a person who challenges you and inspires you, foster that friendship—or one day you may see it slowly disappear or even get terminated.

If you ever get to the point in your life where you feel like someone is not serving you well as a friend, you have the right to choose whether or not to carry on that relationship. Demoting or terminating relationships looks different for everyone. However, if it needs to happen, I want to take a moment and give you full permission to do what you need to do. Keeping someone around who hurts you or brings you down does not serve you in the long run. No rules state that you need to keep anyone in your life who is a negative influence or causing harm. No blood or years put in give anyone the right to bring you down. Take steps to either change the relationship for the better or move forward in life without the negative influence remaining.

This may be a gradual, unintentional process or an immediate, deliberate process, but you are entitled to make these choices in your life. You deserve a life surrounded by individuals who lift you up, create a positive force in your life, and who are intentional about being your friend.

Besides choosing who is in your life, you can also choose to let go of things you're holding onto that don't serve you well. I will be the first to admit that years ago, I struggled hard with holding onto grudges. I still slip up on occasion when I hear someone's name who once upon a time wronged me, and I'll immediately cringe. However, I've also reached the point in my life where I realize there's minimal benefit in holding onto that negativity for someone else.

I think there is something specifically with women—sorry women, but it's true—where that high school mentality creeps into adulthood. I've come across far too many women in my life who, unfortunately, were hurtful for no apparent reason to other women. I don't know why some women feel a need to compete or cut others down so they can rise up, but I've seen it far too often, even as an adult.

One of the hardest things about the time in life when I entered the mental health hospital was hearing all of the rumors and negative comments people made about me. People I didn't even know wounded me deeply by things that eventually trickled back to me.

It took years for me to get over that negativity in my life. Not only did I have to let go of all of the pain I felt from their words, but I also finally chose to forgive every single one of them. In most cases, I didn't have conversations with the other person, but I changed my mindset to let go of the pain.

I've run into many of these people again since that time, and the best thing I've ever done was learn just to smile and say hi. It's fascinating to watch how uncomfortable someone who's done you wrong becomes when they run into you, and you have the guts to look them in the eye and smile.

I've chosen over the years to surround myself with people who didn't need to judge me for my past. Gradually with time, the people who were once judgmental became less and less important in my life until eventually, their opinion just didn't matter in the slightest.

Every person who influences our life will hold weight, but it is up to you to determine how you respond to that influence. If someone hurts me, I can either choose to hold onto that pain and let it eat away at me or decide to take that situation and learn from it. I've learned to take the grudges I've held onto throughout my life and challenge myself to change my mindset about the situation.

One of the most challenging grudges to overcome was against my parents and their choices that affected my life and changed me forever. It would be seemingly easy to sit here and blame my dad for his drug use, claim that he ruined my life, and decide never to talk to him again. If that is how I still viewed what happened, I wouldn't just be holding onto the grudge towards him, but I'd also feel that the pain I felt was irreversible.

I've learned to look at what happened to me as a kid and embrace the lesson that my dad was not evil, and he never intentionally harmed me. My dad was a product of his upbringing, and he was a product of decades of pain and mental illness; his drug use resulted from that. I've learned to see him as a human.

Yes, he "wronged" me, but I've forgiven him and let go of all of that pain that came with it. I've watched him continue to grow and learn from his mistakes. It hasn't been easy, and it hasn't been an overnight process. It's safe to say that forgiving him took years. However, letting go of that grudge has allowed me to view him as a human who made mistakes and made the continuation of our relationship possible.

If you currently hold a grudge toward a person close to you, you are doing nothing but holding onto pain and preventing your relationship from moving forward. Rather than holding onto that negative weight, you have the power to use that grudge to think back and learn about that person. With every grudge I've ever held, I've been able to put myself in that person's place and do everything in my power to empathize with why they made the choices they did. If you think long and hard enough about any situation, I assure you that you will learn something from it. If you can allow yourself to empathize with even the worst of all people who have hurt you, then you will open the doors to learning and growing from each scenario.

Our lives are short, and we are given the gift of meeting new people continuously. It simply is not worth surrounding yourself with anyone who causes you pain or doesn't make you feel good about yourself.

While negativity is powerful and can change a person, positivity is even stronger. More importantly, you are surrounded by those you can learn and grow from to become an even better person. Find people in your life who constantly strive to grow and make those your people. Not only should you learn from them, but you also should feel comfortable challenging those around you to keep growing and becoming better people.

Some of the best people I have learned from in my life are those who have been where I want to go and done things I want to achieve. The days when I am at my best are days when I have genuinely been challenged by someone else to grow, think, or act in a way that I've never before done.

If you want to grow and learn, get out of your comfort zone, have uncomfortable conversations, ask challenging questions, and listen to those who have lessons to teach from their own experiences. This is how change happens, and this is how growth happens, so seek out and embrace these people in your life because they are invaluable beyond belief.

Complete "Rules of the Road"
Rule #5 Activity on **page 111**

A Healthy Body Leads To A Healthy Mind

I preface this entire chapter with the statement that I am, in no way, a nutritionist or a physical fitness expert. I am hardly either of the two, but what I do know is the fact that if you struggle in any way with stress, anxiety, or mental illness, you absolutely need to incorporate exercise and a healthy diet into your daily routine.

When I was at my very lowest of lows, the one piece of advice that I retained was, at least once a day, no matter what, I needed to get outside and walk for a minimum of twenty minutes. That was the condition given. Twenty minutes to walk. Easy, right?

At this time, I was only about twenty-five years old, so I was in that state of life when you can still just get away with eating anything, doing nothing, and somehow you appeared to be in great shape. You know, it's that time in life when everyone in their thirties and above wishes they could go back to because it was so easy and effortless to just be unhealthy without really seeing the repercussions. But even though I may have looked like it at the time, I was not doing anything. I worked long hours, and it was safe to call me a workaholic, so rather than taking the time to focus on my own health, I was instead working my way deeper into my anxiety and depression. I was more focused on just making it day to day and did nothing positive at the time for my own body.

It was at this time that I finally decided to go see a therapist for the very first time. She gave me a homework assignment. The *only* thing I had to do each day—the only thing that actually mattered—was to go outside and walk. Twenty minutes. If I did more, awesome. If I decided to start a physical fitness training program, great. But at the time, that was my bare minimum. And I did it.

Since that time of just the bare minimum, I've gone through the peaks and valleys of physical fitness. As I mentioned earlier, I struggled with an eating disorder. So, part of my relationship with fitness meant sometimes I'd go too far over the other end and become obsessed with working out. Some days on my life's journey, even in my darkest moments, I was more obsessed with how I looked and how far I ran that day than anything else in my life.

If anyone has been through the extremes of physical fitness, it's me. I know what it's like not to be able to get out of bed and not be able even to fathom the hardship of walking for twenty minutes outside. At one time in my life, the thought of that could make me cry. But I also know what it's like to become so obsessed with physical fitness that running ten miles was not enough for one day.

My challenge was learning how to find balance in my physical fitness (Balance, by the way, is another intention word I'm still constantly working on in my life). Not only that, but I had to eat the right way to support what I was doing physically. And food for me is just another hot topic that I could genuinely write an entire book about if I wanted. My battle with food has been lifelong, and even though I haven't actively struggled with or engaged in any eating disorders since before having children, the internal battle still looms almost daily for me.

My unhealthy relationship with eating started at a very young age. I learned that food was a comfort when I needed support. I remember being bullied at the age of seven or eight because of my weight. I was not over-weight, but I was bullied nonetheless. Kids are just cruel. I was standing on my childhood street, eating some sort of coffee cake, one of my favorites at the time. My neighbor called me "Sara Lee" and knocked the piece out of my hand, telling me I shouldn't be eating that because I was already fat.

I'm sure this kid grew up to be a very nice guy; hopefully, he is happily married and teaches his children to be kind to one another. But man, back on Arthur Avenue in 1990, he ingrained a pattern in my head that stuck with me for decades. I learned to eat when I was unhappy and eat when I was alone, and when I got to high school and life took a tailspin out of con-trol, I somehow taught myself to cope using the opposite methods.

They say eating disorders stem from a lack of control in your life, so I took the already negative association with food and used it as the only thing I could control while the rest of my life as a teenager ran rampant. I bounced back and forth for at least a decade between anorexia and buli-mia—often paired with exercise obsession. My eating habits, or lack there-of, also befriended intense binge drinking, which left me with many nights I cannot remember.

When I think back to what I was doing to my body, it's a miracle I survived. I was not feeding it enough food—if I fed it any at all—and then I abused alcohol to the point where my body shut down on more than one occasion. But in the world of high school or college, all of this went unnoticed.

At that time, I was one of many girls drinking and passing out, so it wasn't really on anyone's radar. As I've already mentioned, instead of being horrified by our behavior, we laughed at the funny stories from the night before, making it all that much easier to cover up my struggles. The reality of the situation was that I was treated my body in a very unhealthy manner. In turn, my mental health got worse. I was more focused on what I looked like than what I felt or acted like.

For me, getting and staying mentally healthy is so connected to my physical health that I cannot even talk about one without the other. If you are a person who has never struggled with an eating disorder, then definitely take a moment and consider yourself lucky. Freedom from eating disorders is a bonus to maintaining a healthy lifestyle. While not everyone struggles with physical health to an extreme, your mental and physical health are completely intertwined. To work on one without working on the other is really a contradiction and will certainly slow your progress.

I've reached a point in my life where healthy eating and exercise are an integration of overall mindfulness. I am intentional about doing both. An abundance of research supports this approach. I recommend you do your own research when it comes to details as far as diet and exercise. However, what I really want to emphasize is that both should be mindful decisions.

When it comes to food, I generally eat a plant-based diet and try to eat food in its most basic form. I love vegetables and make sure my family eats just as many veggies as possible. I'm also all about ingredients. The fewer ingredients in something, the better. The fewer artificially manufactured ingredients, the better. My overall mentality is that eating fast food, fried foods, and sugary foods and drinks are not completely banned in all forms but instead are eaten rarely and in moderation.

I try to achieve balance, so I have found that diets do not and cannot work for me. I've learned to create eating patterns that feel healthy and are viable long-term.

As for working out and generally being active, my focus is similar to food; it's all about balance. While I have gone through phases of intense exercise and gotten in great shape off and on, it is more important for me to be consistent and enjoy what I'm doing when it comes to physical fitness. I make it a goal to do something active every single day. Some days that's a trip to the gym, a workout DVD, or a yoga class, but some days I simply walk around the neighborhood with my family.

I love to set goals for myself and achieve them, so one of the best ways to achieve my physical activity goals is by creating a plan and sticking to it. I've run marathons, done mud run challenges, and done other physical fitness challenges. The important thing, for me, is staying active. When I find myself struggling, I know I need to step it up as far as fitness goals. I know working out isn't everyone's cup of tea, but there are so many ways to stay active, and I encourage you to think outside the box if you are a person who cringes at the thought of exercise.

Part of actively achieving happiness is challenging yourself and doing things you've never done before, and that couldn't be any more true than finding an exercise routine that works for you. Regardless of your experience, I am giving you the same challenge my therapist gave me over a decade ago—take a walk around the block. Every day. Twenty minutes a day. That's it. That's my bare minimum challenge to you.

A response to this challenge looks different for everyone. For some of you, maybe you'll laugh at that because it seems so easy, and that's okay. If you are inclined to a more intense physical fitness routine, then, by all means, keep it going and go strong! Just make sure that you are doing it for the right reasons and you are mindful of how your activity is affecting your body.

Are you drinking enough water throughout the workout and day overall? Are you eating clean and nutritious foods that aid your body in your workouts? The goal is not just to achieve a workout plan but also to be sure you are fueling your body appropriately so that your mind can also benefit.

If you are anything like me, one straightforward addition to your plan can make it more successful—adding an accountability partner. Anytime I am on my game and doing well, I have someone doing it with me. Whether it is a workout plan or an eating plan, I almost always have at least one other friend or person I talk to almost daily about what I am doing. My husband is almost always on board for a good old-fashioned fitness competition. It's become one other thing we've done together that helps both of us stay healthy and get out of any fitness or food slumps. It is also a way to bond and work together to achieve a goal. Find a friend who is reading this book too, and maybe that's a good starting point.

Ideally, you will come to a place where exercise and eating healthy is not a chore but part of your daily routine. It becomes second nature. If you're doing it with the right mindset, it really can become something enjoyable. Now, most of the time, I look forward to working out. I've learned to eat foods that serve my body, and in turn, I feel good about myself and my habits.

Like everything else I've stated, this is still and probably always will be an area where I have to actively work to stay healthy. It still doesn't come naturally for me, and it probably never will. Still, at this point, I am happy with my body, and more than anything—and maybe this just comes with age—I am grateful that I am still here and physically able to do anything and everything I want with my body. Many people aren't that lucky. Ninety-nine percent of us take our health entirely for granted, and it isn't until it is taken away from us that we suddenly realize how good we once had it.

A healthy body does not arise from solely food, water, and exercise. Outside of physical fitness and eating habits, we can do so many little things to achieve overall wellness. I wish I could make it a rule for everyone reading this book to get a dog, but I'm not sure it works like that, and actually, dogs are a ton of work.

But if you've ever owned a pet, you already know the benefit. There's something pretty magical about cuddling a dog—or a cat if that's your jam. Pet ownership is scientifically proven to improve your health by lowering your blood pressure, cholesterol, and feelings of loneliness. It also increases your opportunities for exercise, outdoor activity, and socialization.

Maybe you're not an animal person, and that's okay—it's not a mandatory part of the course, so you're in the clear.

But we all have these moments in life when, if we're trying, we can find the good in any situation. These don't have to be big things, but you can always find something or someone to be grateful for in life. Even in the worst of the worst and the lowest of the lows, you can find joy if you allow yourself to do so.

Snuggle a baby, pet a dog, make a fresh batch of coffee—that smell is perfection, even if you don't drink coffee—take a hot bath, go to your favorite store and stroll the aisles, book a vacation, plan a night out with friends, go to a sporting event, or watch your favorite movie.

Though I've still not mastered breathing and meditation as a daily practice, I quickly learned that they are tremendous stress relievers—especially if you are in a state of panic or anxiety—they can have a huge, lasting difference on your overall mood. But if you are anything like me, you probably rarely think about your breathing, especially when you're stressed or overwhelmed. Being mindful when you are upset or emotional has a profound influence on your ability to calm down quickly.

Like identifying any other triggers that set you off, if you can identify how your body physically responds to stress, then slowing down and correcting your physical response will be that much easier. Even right now, as you read this, think about your jaw. Is it clenched? Probably. Are your shoulders tense? I bet they are. When we're driving, reading, or sitting at a desk and working, our bodies are naturally more tense than relaxed. How bizarre that we have to train ourselves to be calm?

It takes practice and patience, and trust me, I'm still working on it, but even something as simple as a breathing app on your phone or the breathing reminder on your watch can be useful for overall physical health.

And finally, the very last piece that I cannot leave out when it comes to talking about a healthy body is faith. I hesitated to bring this up because so many ranges of faith and methods of belief exist. The last thing I would ever want to do is alienate you on your journey because we believe in different things. Personally, I have gone through big waves in my faith journey.

I was raised a Lutheran and brought up attending church my entire life. To me, especially as I reached high school, church was a place where I felt comfortable. I made solid friendships there, and I enjoyed things like mission trips, lock-ins, pool parties, and all sorts of other fun youth group events. I became close with many people at our church, but I don't think I ever really became fully connected to anything spiritually at all. At the time, I mostly just viewed it as another way to make friends and distract myself from all the other stuff going on in my life.

During my college years, I started questioning what I believed and why. I spent the first eighteen years of my life just going through the motions, and while I believed in God, I didn't even know what that meant for me. From college on, my viewpoint changed and evolved. I now have a deeper understanding of spirituality, and I believe in a higher power that is bigger and greater than any of us can understand.

When I talk with people about God, a concern that often arises is that people who have a different belief system than mine feel a sense of division. Rather than focusing on the similarities of faith, it seems many people cannot get past the differences between different religious institutions. Having a productive conversation isn't always feasible.

If I am going to label my religious beliefs, I am currently and have been a lifelong Christian. Over the past fifteen years, this is an intentional decision I made for myself instead of blindly following my parents' practices. I am a firm believer that everyone needs to have their own spiritual journey. Through my journey, I've questioned just about everything.

I've questioned science, the history of the Bible, and I've even researched religions outside of Christianity because I find all of it fascinating. Ultimately, I've come to believe that no matter what religion or spiritual form you practice—or whether you practice one at all—the actual effort of intentionally contemplating your faith and what that means to you is extremely useful in your journey towards health. If you don't know what you believe, that's okay. I didn't know for a long time, and I still have internal thoughts about where I stand on certain spiritual notions.

I know one thing for sure. Sometimes when you go through a tough time, questioning your faith and wondering why this is happening to you is completely normal and okay. I found that when I lost my mother-in-law, I once again began questioning life and the why's behind it. Even for someone who deeply practices their faith, when terrible circumstances are beyond your control, it is exceptionally challenging to rationalize why God or whatever higher power you believe in would put you in the situation. But it was through my faith in God that I came to my own answer to this question and made peace with her death.

My faith has gotten me through so much of my hardest times in life, and even though your picture of spirituality may look entirely different than mine, I encourage you to lean into it. Work on defining it for yourself.

By questioning these things and looking deep within yourself to find the answers, you help yourself find balance. You begin to see the answer to one of life's greatest questions, which is, "Why are we here?"

I certainly don't have the answer to this question, and that's my point. I think it is part of every person's journey to figure that out for themselves. If you find yourself struggling with life's day-to-day routines—whether you practice religion or not—it's imperative in those times, more than any others, to figure out for yourself where you stand. These are hard questions, and you may not even be able to answer them, but the important thing is to think about it. As you contemplate these questions, you actually may find that you develop faith in something that you didn't have faith in before.

I know that by questioning life's challenges, you may discover a faith. I do not doubt that discovering faith can help you move forward. When you ever find yourself truly lost, having someone or something greater than you to look up to can be healing, powerful, and transformational.

Complete "Rules of the Road"
Rule #6 Activity on **page 119**

Never Stop Working

If you've made it this far and take anything away from these lessons, let it be this. If you sincerely want to change your life and improve your happiness, reading this book and doing a few exercises will not change you. However, what will change you is constantly revisiting some of these principles and lessons and never stopping your work on them. The ebbs and flows of happiness are inevitable.

One of the hardest things for me about putting continual effort into moving forward—despite any of the trauma or bad experiences I've had in my past—is overcoming the concept that my past defines me.

It has taken me years, almost a decade, to come to the total realization that I am not defined by my past. My wrongdoings do not define me. Those actions do not make up who I am in life now.

Was that a version of me? Yes. That version did exist. Am I proud of everything I've done, the people I've hurt, the relationships I've lost? No. I am definitely not proud of all of that, but more than anything, those actions do not define me.

Again, let me say it for those of you in the far back of the room, *no matter what your past or even current situation looks like, it does not define you.*

I am in charge of the narrative of my life. I am in control of my identity, and nobody else can claim that responsibility but me. Even at my lowest of lows and my absolute rock bottoms in life, it was up to me how I handled those situations.

If you find yourself in a place you're not quite proud of, give yourself a little grace and understanding. Never will this moment represent who you are as a person, but it is instead a roadblock in your journey.

I am also not defined by my diagnosis, nor do I believe anyone with any diagnosis out there should be. A person living with cancer is not defined solely as a person with cancer. A person with Down syndrome is not solely defined as a person with Down syndrome. Do those diagnoses play major parts in their lives? Absolutely. But by no means does it determine their identity.

Mental health is just that. It is a piece of a person's identity. Every person on this planet is on the mental health spectrum in one way or another. We all have good days, and we all have bad days. We all have rough patches of life, and we all have patches of life where we live on top of the world. Those moments, those emotional highs and lows, and even those labels we attach to people are just glimpses into what makes a whole person.

I've finally gotten to the point—though again, this has taken years in the making—where I can finally openly speak about my past and my struggles with mental illness. But even more than that, I think that anyone who gets to this point—goes through hardships, goes through trauma, and somehow comes out on the other side— has a responsibility to society to speak about the lessons learned through our trials.

This certainly doesn't mean that everyone who goes through something needs to write a book—though being someone who works in the industry, I certainly think everyone's story has value enough to write one—but each of us has a responsibility to own lessons learned and then help others move forward in life.

There are so many platforms where your own candidness and honesty in lessons learned could help someone. It can be as simple as commenting on a thread on social media, having an open and honest conversation at a dinner table, or speaking up with a friend or in a classroom. The more we can normalize a spectrum of happiness being a journey and not a destination, the easier it will be for people to discover their own happiness.

Not only can we accept our own mistakes or character flaws as pieces of us rather than what defines us, but the more we can also start to accept one another's flaws and mistakes and look at the whole person. So keep having these honest conversations moving forward—not just with yourself but also with your friends, family, and coworkers. The more transparent you are, the more success you will have at finding this happiness.

We've found ourselves in this society that is so quick to judge each other, especially those in the public spotlight, based on their actions, without even remotely knowing their whole picture. What if the next time you saw a news headline of a person who made a mistake, whatever that mistake may have been or no matter how severe it was, and before you judged that person and wrote them off, what if you thought for a minute about what type of past led them to that point in life? What did they go through, and what was their narrative that we had no idea about that was running through their head?

The same grace I ask that you give yourself in saying, "My choices do not define me," I ask that you also extend that grace to everyone you meet. Embrace the understanding that we all make mistakes in life. So before we rush out and write off someone else's narrative, stop and flip it in your mind.

Lead with grace. Don't write their narrative for others, but see that we are all on unique roads to finding our own happiness. Be open to learning about where each individual is coming from in life and let that be the light in which you see them.

Each of us is trying to move forward in the best way we can with the path we were given. Intersections in life look quite different for each of us on this journey. Though it looks different for everyone, we all ultimately have the same goal in mind, and we all are facing different struggles and trying to overcome some narrative we've ultimately written for ourselves in life.

Whether today is day one or day five-thousand-and-one on this journey for you, you are here on a new road. Fresh pavement. You are the driver; you are in control. You get to wake up every day with the intention that you can achieve happiness today.

It is not a destination. Nobody is going to be waiting at the gates with that fruity cocktail in hand. This is it. You own it. It starts now. With every encounter you have moving forward, keep this intention in mind.

Your success in life will not define it, and even more so, your mistakes will not define it. You create your life, every single day, one little step at a time, and guess what? Every single day, no matter how much you screw it up the day before, you get to keep going and try again. You get to keep working. You get a fresh start every twenty-four hours. It's kind of cool. So own it, embrace it, and don't ever stop driving towards it.

This is the end for me, but in the spirit of what I've been preaching here, I am leaving you with a continuing workbook to complete on your own after you're done reading. There are yearly and monthly goals, and there is so much for you to work on and think about moving forward. Save this workbook, revisit these topics as often as needed, and keep in mind that your answers may even change for some of these questions after a few months, so it is worth revisiting.

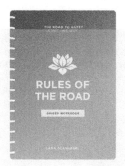

Complete "Rules of the Road"
Rule #7 Activity on **page 123**

ACKNOWLEDGMENTS

Brian, through the ups and the downs, thank you for always being there for me. Thank you for standing by my side when I needed you the most. Thank you for sticking up for me when nobody else in life would. Thank you for supporting my dreams and always being in my corner with them, no matter how crazy I may sometimes sound. You are my rock, and I will always, no matter where life takes us, see you as the guiding light to helping me escape the complete darkness that once surrounded me, and for that, I am forever grateful.

Mom, you are officially my longest-running best friend in life. You have taught me what strength in the face of adversity looks like. You are the strongest person I know, and I am honored to call you my mother. You have made me the woman I am today, and I will always look up to you for how you taught me to love unconditionally.

Dad, I am so incredibly proud of you in every way. You've taught me how to never stop fighting and how to never give up on yourself, even when everyone else gave up on you. I admire the way you always look to help others through your own experiences. This book, and my desire to help others, is because of your passion for doing so in life.

To my family and friends, you all know who you are. I will never be able to thank you for loving me at my worst, for seeing through the bad and knowing that good existed within me, and sticking with me through all of the adversity that I faced, and in turn, brought you through with me. I've been so lucky to not only have the most amazing family but to have married into a family whose love is so strong that I am here today because of all of you as well. Thank you to you all for loving me for me.

I dedicate this book to the loving memory of my amazing queen bee, Dianna Marie (Chibucos) Glashagel. You entered my life in the storm, and you saw me through until your very last day, hugging and kissing and butting your way into our lives in a way that I only could truly appreciate once you were gone. You taught me how to live and lead my family as a mother with grace, poise, respect, dignity, and love. I will forever love you, mama.

RULES OF
THE ROAD

66

Put blinders on to those things that conspire to hold you back, especially the ones in your own head.

MERYL STREEP

Stop Comparing.

Comparison Is the Thief of Joy

Name three people you've envied in the past. For each person, write what about them you envied. After thinking about it, how do you feel?

Person 1

Person 2

Person 3

Now for each person, think about his or her life. Write something you think she or he may struggle with. Or consider the possibility that he or she has challenges you don't know about because they have been kept hidden.

Person 1

Person 2

Person 3

What steps can you take in the next month to focus on your own goals and happiness? What will you do to remove your sense of comparison to others?

Be Honest With Yourself

List the top five things that contribute to your happiness. Next, write your why for each.

1

2

3

4

5

Now list the top five things that take away from your happiness. What have you done in the past to deal with your unhappiness? How can you turn things around? Be honest with yourself about how you can change your life for the better.

1 ....

2 ....

3 ....

4 ....

5 ....

When you read back what you wrote, you should be able to identify some triggers for your unhappiness and anxiety. Take a look at your statements identify your top triggers for each below. For each, write down how you can catch and work with that trigger before it becomes an issue.

If you are being honest with yourself, part of that is being able to identify your own strengths. Take some time to reflect on your strengths; write down your top three. Next, for each one, write how you can use it to your advantage and how you envision it adding to happiness in your life, career, relationships, etc.

Be Honest With Those You Love

Below, list your allies. Who do you trust? Who can you talk to? Who talks to you that is looking to be heard and doesn't want advice? How can you best serve this person as their ally?

66

They always say time changes things,
but you actually have to change
them yourself.

ANDY WARHOL

Find What Fulfills You And Do More Of It

What are you passionate about? What makes you happy? List everything you can think of. Just do a mind-dump here. Truly, list anything and everything.

How often do you do the things you listed? Is it enough? If not, what barriers are in your way?

Create an intention word or statement by working through a few goal statements. This may seem repetitive as you're doing the exercise, but force yourself to think about what fulfills you and how you can get there. All of the credit here goes to one of my coworkers. He leads our team in an intention-statement meeting once a week, and every week, I find that my statements grow deeper and deeper and truer to my true intentions and desires.

Start with a goal you are working towards, either professionally, personally, or both. With each following statement, think about why you want to achieve that goal. Think deeply about your reasons and what you really are trying to achieve. Keep going, and with every "I want," dig a little deeper. We will end with your word here, I promise. Complete the following sentences:

I want ....

....

....

....

Because I want ....

....

....

Because I want ....

....

....

Because I want ....

....

....

Because I want ....

....

....

After you have completed as many of these "I want" statements as you can, and you feel like you've gotten to your root, then read through them one more time, and think of one word that encompasses this idea and can help you get there.

WRITE THAT WORD OR STATEMENT HERE:

This is your intention word. Now write this word or statement down somewhere outside of this book. Put it somewhere that you will see it regularly and can use as a constant reminder of these goals. Revisit this word as often as you want. Maybe your goals will even change throughout the year, and that's okay. You can always come back and re-do this exercise and change it as often as possible. Hopefully, each time you do this exercise, you gain more clarity about your goals, and in turn, your intentions.

Now to embody this intention statement, you will need to take action steps. List at least three action steps you can take this month to move towards your intention statement or word.

Think about a time in your life when you waited for something to happen that you perceived would ultimately make you happy. What happened when that time came?

Was there ever a time when you thought success would bring you happiness? When you achieved that success, how did you feel? Think long term. Maybe this was a promotion you received. Don't think about the time right after the promotion when you felt that immediate relief and happiness, but think past that. Once you got into the flow of things again, how did your feelings change?

Think of where you are right now in life. List all the things that bring you happiness right now.

What can you use to remind yourself daily to be grateful or happy about these things in your life? Come up with a plan of at least one way to create a visual reminder of this—journal (see the end of the book), bulletin board, cell phone, fridge, computer, note on the mirror.

Make it a point to put these reminders somewhere that you can easily view them. Remember to glance at them now and then. Sometimes we need to be reminded of how lucky we are.

Surround Yourself With People Who Make You Better

List the most important people in your life, and for each person, write how they add value and challenge you. Think of your friends, but if you'd like, include important family members.

Now, consider this same list of people. How do you add value to each of their lives? Have you ever communicated with them how important they are to you? If not, why not?

Whether the people you listed are friends or family, I highly suggest that you make it very clear to each of them how important they are and how they add meaning and value to your life.

If you struggled to come up with ways in which you add value to their lives, ponder it further. Do you fully listen when they talk? Do you help them when they are in need? Are you equal partners in your friendship? Do you put their feelings at the forefront of your relationship? Do you challenge them in life? Do you inspire them? Do you cheer for their accomplishments or compete with them?

Write your thoughts below. Be honest with yourself. And if you find you don't have a whole lot to write about regarding the value you add to their lives, now is your chance to change that.

Next, think about the people in your life whose names you did not write on this list. Why isn't their name there? Take some time to think about and evaluate that friendship. What value does this person add to your life? Is this person more of a negative influence than a positive? Is this person also putting forth effort in the relationship? Does this person add stress to your life? Write your thoughts below.

Once you have taken this time to fully evaluate the most important people in your life, switch gears and think for a second about the people in your life with whom you hold grudges. Maybe these people are currently in your life, perhaps you wrote about them above, or maybe this person is no longer in your life.

You know what I'm going to ask you to do here; you've got the idea by now. Consider any grudges you currently hold. Maybe this is a person you are still close with today, or maybe this is someone who is no longer in your life. Put yourself in the other person's shoes. Where were they coming from? What can you learn from them? Think back to the situation; is there something you didn't know at the time or that you still don't know? What could this person have been going through to have caused them to hurt you once upon a time?

If you have not already done so, how can you forgive this person? Is it something you can communicate with them about or openly discuss to move forward in your relationship? Or is this a person that you will not or cannot see any more in the future, and forgiving them isn't going to be about a conversation, but rather an acknowledgment on your end of past action, and all you can do now is move forward with that lesson in mind. What can you learn moving forward in relationships by letting go of these grudges?

Letting go of the weight of any of this negativity in your life—whether it is a grudge or a relationship that no longer serves you—you make more room in your life for good. You deserve good people, and they deserve the good within you in return. Write how you plan to bring out the best in people moving forward in your relationships and how you can be open to letting them bring out the best in you.

"

*The two most important days
in your life are the day you are born
and the day you find out why.*

MARK TWAIN

A Healthy Body Leads To A Healthy Mind

What do you struggle with as far as food and exercise?

Do you notice a mood shift when you eat healthfully and exercise regularly? If so, have you ever been in a good pattern as far as eating being physically healthy? I am not asking about a diet or workout plan here, rather prompting a general awareness of eating habits and physical activity. If so, describe what that looked like for you and where you were as far as overall mood and happiness at that time.

Come up with your nutrition and daily activity plan. Start with one month at a time. What are your goals? What is your area of focus and why? Before actually grabbing a calendar and mapping it out, think about how you will approach this and your reasons for doing so.

Do you have a buddy who can help you achieve these goals by either doing the workouts with you or who is committed to rooting you on? Who could you ask? How could they also benefit from this challenge? Your goal is twofold—twenty minutes a day minimum of physical activity and contemplate what you can modify your diet to make it healthier for the long-term.

List every "thing" (not people, you already did that) in your life you are grateful for—big or small, it doesn't matter, just dump all of the things here. Think outside of the box. List at least ten items, but I know you can do more than that...

List at least five things you can do to break a trend when you're having a bad day. Copy this list and post it somewhere visible.

What does faith mean to you? What does your faith look like? How can you lean into your faith when you are lost or stuck?

Never Stop Working

What is the narrative of your life that you have written for yourself, and you are officially going to throw away because this will no longer define you?

We're not done!

Now follow along with me here...throw that "narrative" away—not literally, of course, I want you to keep the book! Though I will say if you want to go all out, and I highly suggest you do, write that statement of your past narrative on a separate sheet of paper, and by all means, throw that paper in a fire pit. It does not define you any longer. You are not that person. Those are choices you've made; those are pieces of your past, those are bits of you, and that is simply a small piece of your story.

**You're done reading the book,
but the work is not done....**

ONE-YEAR
MINDFULNESS
JOURNAL

Enacting change takes work, lots of hard work, and you are the only one capable of doing this work. If you wait around for someone else to change, or you wait for circumstances to be just right, you may be in for a rude awakening. It's like wanting to get in shape, making a plan, and then not following through. Having a good plan is excellent, but following through and putting in the work is all that matters.

Part of choosing happiness is finding it all around you, and this requires some mindfulness and gratitude on your part. Anyone can find the bad in life. That part is easy. The hard part is finding the good. The more you do it, the easier it becomes. Keeping a journal is an amazing way to reflect on the past, set goals for the future, and live a happier life.

Journaling, or what some experts refer to as expressive writing, is one of the most beneficial things you can do for your mind and body, even if it's just for a few minutes a day. Research shows that simply putting pen to paper can help people process and heal from trauma, reduce stress, and even boost immune response.

Even if you're a professional writer, it's so easy to draw a blank when staring down at a blank page. With the sheer amount of distractions in life, I never found it easy to write about something daily. I preferred to use prompts. Take a few minutes every day to set aside time to write. Don't think about grammar or spelling or what anyone else would think.

This journal is just for you. Use it to start thinking in a new way. Start finding gratitude in the small things, and start expressing your thoughts and emotions so you can continue to learn and grow from them. Use this journal as often as you want. You can write one prompt a day, a couple a week, and revisit them as often as you'd like.

Yearly Goal-Setting

Since we can't always start from square one, let's start this journal as close to the beginning as possible—pretend New Year's eve! I don't care what the date is, but let's do a little new year resolution and goal-setting. I don't call these resolutions; I prefer goals. You can come back and adjust these as often as you want.

Revisit these goals in about six months, just to check progress, and then again in a year. If the real new year comes around, that's an excellent opportunity to spot-check them, as well. Ultimately, it's important that you keep these goals at the top of your mind, and if you do feel like you need to make changes, that is more than okay.

WRITE TODAY'S DATE:

_____

Put a reminder in your calendar for six months from now to check in on these goals, and then again in a year from today.

INTENTION FOR THE YEAR

You've already written an intention word or statement,
so feel free to copy that here:

List your top three career or monetary goals for the year:

1 ....
....

2 ....
....

3 ....
....

List three things you are going to stop doing this year:

1 ....
....

2 ....
....

3 ....
....

List three things you are going to do more of this year:

1 ....
....

2 ....
....

3 ....
....

List three bucket list items you want to do this year:

1 ....

....

2 ....

....

3 ....

....

What obstacles might derail you in achieving any of these goals, and how will you get around them?

What do you hope to gain from journaling regularly?

MONTHLY GOALS

At the beginning of each month, choose at least three goals you would like to achieve. At the end of the month, revisit these and cross off the ones you achieved. Plan the next month accordingly.

MONTH:

GOAL 1   **GOAL 2**   **GOAL 3**

MONTH:

GOAL 1   **GOAL 2**   **GOAL 3**

MONTH:

GOAL 1   **GOAL 2**   **GOAL 3**

MONTH:

GOAL 1	GOAL 2	GOAL 3

MONTH:

GOAL 1	GOAL 2	GOAL 3

MONTH:

GOAL 1	GOAL 2	GOAL 3

MONTH:

GOAL 1   GOAL 2   GOAL 3

MONTH:

GOAL 1   GOAL 2   GOAL 3

MONTH:

GOAL 1   GOAL 2   GOAL 3

MONTH:

GOAL 1	GOAL 2	GOAL 3

MONTH:

GOAL 1	GOAL 2	GOAL 3

MONTH:

GOAL 1	GOAL 2	GOAL 3

POSITIVE AFFIRMATIONS

Reciting positive things about yourself helps you reframe negative thoughts. Think of what you want to invite into your life, and write some of these down. Keep them short and simple. Start with the words "I am" and include a verb ending in "-ing." Example: "I am working my hardest to achieve the goals I never thought possible" or "I am stronger than I have ever given myself credit for." Also "I can" statements such as, "I can get any job I want if I really work for it."

A LETTER TO YOUR FUTURE SELF

Pick a specific date when you will open it. Envision where you'll be and what your hopes for yourself are.

APOLOGIES

Write a note to someone in your life who you have hurt. What would you like to say to them? If you feel inclined, send this letter. Think about it, what is the worst that could happen?

SIMPLE PLEASURES

What song do you always play to cheer you up? What makes it comforting?

What TV show makes you happy? Why do you love it?

What movie? What about it do you love?

Where is your favorite place to be? Why do you love it so much?

What is your favorite comfort food? Why do you love it so much?

*Intentionally make it a point to incorporate these things into your life way more often than you already are.

EXPRESSING THANKS

Write a thank-you note to someone who has had a positive influence on your life. You can choose to send this to the person or just save it—though I encourage you to consider sending it.

BUCKET LIST

What are the top five things you've always wanted to do in life?

1 ....

2 ....

3 ....

4 ....

5 ....

How can you make these happen? Which do you plan to do this year? How will doing these make you feel?

SELF LOVE

Compliment yourself on **your intelligence**:

Compliment yourself on **your looks**:

Compliment yourself on **your personality**:

Compliment yourself on **your generosity**:

Compliment yourself on **your kindness toward yourself and others**:

What is your "superpower" in life? How can you use this to your advantage in your relationships and career?

ME TIME

What does the idea of self-care mean to you? What activities does it involve?

How can you incorporate these into your daily routine?

DREAM A LITTLE DREAM

Describe your vision for your ideal world. What are your wishes for the people around you? What relationships do you have? What do your surroundings look like? What do you do for fun?

GRATITUDE JOURNAL

Attitude of Gratitude 30-Day Journal

Take five minutes every morning and five minutes every night to fill out these quick prompts. I also encourage you to come back and read these regularly.

I have included thirty days of a gratitude journal for you, but if you are looking to continue this past thirty days, go to my website for a free printable download. You can choose to use these daily for thirty days or just as needed for a pick-me-up in gratitude.

MORNING JOURNALING

I am grateful for: ....

....

....

because ....

....

My focus/priorities for today: ....

....

....

....

EVENING JOURNALING

The best part of my day was ....

....

....

....

How did I get better or make someone better today? ....

....

....

....

MORNING JOURNALING

I am grateful for: ....

....

....

because ....

....

My focus/priorities for today: ....

....

....

....

....

EVENING JOURNALING

The best part of my day was ....

....

....

....

....

How did I get better or make someone better today? ....

....

....

....

MORNING JOURNALING

I am grateful for: ....

....

....

because ....

....

My focus/priorities for today: ....

....

....

....

....

EVENING JOURNALING

The best part of my day was ....

....

....

....

....

How did I get better or make someone better today? ....

....

....

....

MORNING JOURNALING

I am grateful for: ....

....

....

because ....

....

My focus/priorities for today: ....

....

....

....

....

EVENING JOURNALING

The best part of my day was ....

....

....

....

....

How did I get better or make someone better today? ....

....

....

....

MORNING JOURNALING

I am grateful for: ....

....

....

because ....

....

My focus/priorities for today: ....

....

....

....

....

EVENING JOURNALING

The best part of my day was ....

....

....

....

....

How did I get better or make someone better today? ....

....

....

MORNING JOURNALING

I am grateful for: ....

....

....

because ....

....

My focus/priorities for today: ....

....

....

....

....

EVENING JOURNALING

The best part of my day was ....

....

....

....

How did I get better or make someone better today? ....

....

....

MORNING JOURNALING

I am grateful for: ....

....

....

because ....

....

My focus/priorities for today: ....

....

....

....

....

EVENING JOURNALING

The best part of my day was ....

....

....

....

....

How did I get better or make someone better today? ....

....

....

....

MORNING JOURNALING

I am grateful for: ....

....

....

because ....

....

My focus/priorities for today: ....

....

....

....

....

EVENING JOURNALING

The best part of my day was ....

....

....

....

....

How did I get better or make someone better today? ....

....

....

....

MORNING JOURNALING

I am grateful for: ....

....

....

because ....

....

My focus/priorities for today: ....

....

....

....

....

EVENING JOURNALING

The best part of my day was ....

....

....

....

How did I get better or make someone better today? ....

....

....

....

MORNING JOURNALING

I am grateful for: ....

....

....

because ....

....

My focus/priorities for today: ....

....

....

....

....

EVENING JOURNALING

The best part of my day was ....

....

....

....

....

How did I get better or make someone better today? ....

....

....

....

MORNING JOURNALING

I am grateful for: ....

....

....

because ....

....

My focus/priorities for today: ....

....

....

....

....

EVENING JOURNALING

The best part of my day was ....

....

....

....

....

How did I get better or make someone better today? ....

....

....

....

MORNING JOURNALING

I am grateful for: ....

....

....

because ....

....

My focus/priorities for today: ....

....

....

....

....

EVENING JOURNALING

The best part of my day was ....

....

....

....

....

How did I get better or make someone better today? ....

....

....

....

MORNING JOURNALING

I am grateful for: ....

....

....

because ....

....

My focus/priorities for today: ....

....

....

....

....

EVENING JOURNALING

The best part of my day was ....

....

....

....

....

How did I get better or make someone better today? ....

....

....

....

MORNING JOURNALING

I am grateful for: ....

....

....

because ....

....

My focus/priorities for today: ....

....

....

....

....

EVENING JOURNALING

The best part of my day was ....

....

....

....

....

How did I get better or make someone better today? ....

....

....

....

MORNING JOURNALING

I am grateful for: ....

....

....

because ....

....

My focus/priorities for today: ....

....

....

....

....

EVENING JOURNALING

The best part of my day was ....

....

....

....

....

How did I get better or make someone better today? ....

....

....

....

MORNING JOURNALING

I am grateful for: ....

....

....

because ....

....

My focus/priorities for today: ....

....

....

....

....

EVENING JOURNALING

The best part of my day was ....

....

....

....

How did I get better or make someone better today? ....

....

....

....

MORNING JOURNALING

I am grateful for: ....

....

....

because ....

....

My focus/priorities for today: ....

....

....

....

....

EVENING JOURNALING

The best part of my day was ....

....

....

....

....

How did I get better or make someone better today? ....

....

....

....

MORNING JOURNALING

I am grateful for: ....
....
....

because ....
....

My focus/priorities for today: ....
....
....
....
....

EVENING JOURNALING

The best part of my day was ....
....
....
....
....

How did I get better or make someone better today? ....
....
....
....

MORNING JOURNALING

I am grateful for: ....

....

....

because ....

....

My focus/priorities for today: ....

....

....

....

....

EVENING JOURNALING

The best part of my day was ....

....

....

....

....

How did I get better or make someone better today? ....

....

....

....

MORNING JOURNALING

I am grateful for: ....

....

....

because ....

....

My focus/priorities for today: ....

....

....

....

....

EVENING JOURNALING

The best part of my day was ....

....

....

....

....

How did I get better or make someone better today? ....

....

....

....

MORNING JOURNALING

I am grateful for: ....

....

....

because ....

....

My focus/priorities for today: ....

....

....

....

....

EVENING JOURNALING

The best part of my day was ....

....

....

....

....

How did I get better or make someone better today? ....

....

....

....

MORNING JOURNALING

I am grateful for: ....

....

....

because ....

....

My focus/priorities for today: ....

....

....

....

....

EVENING JOURNALING

The best part of my day was ....

....

....

....

....

How did I get better or make someone better today? ....

....

....

....

MORNING JOURNALING

I am grateful for: ....

....

....

because ....

....

My focus/priorities for today: ....

....

....

....

....

EVENING JOURNALING

The best part of my day was ....

....

....

....

How did I get better or make someone better today? ....

....

....

....

MORNING JOURNALING

I am grateful for: ....

....

....

because ....

....

My focus/priorities for today: ....

....

....

....

....

EVENING JOURNALING

The best part of my day was ....

....

....

....

....

How did I get better or make someone better today? ....

....

....

....

MORNING JOURNALING

I am grateful for: ....

....

....

because ....

....

My focus/priorities for today: ....

....

....

....

....

EVENING JOURNALING

The best part of my day was ....

....

....

....

....

How did I get better or make someone better today? ....

....

....

....

DATE:

MORNING JOURNALING

I am grateful for: ....

....

....

because ....

....

My focus/priorities for today: ....

....

....

....

....

EVENING JOURNALING

The best part of my day was ....

....

....

....

How did I get better or make someone better today? ....

....

....

MORNING JOURNALING

I am grateful for: ....

....

....

because ....

....

My focus/priorities for today: ....

....

....

....

....

EVENING JOURNALING

The best part of my day was ....

....

....

....

....

How did I get better or make someone better today? ....

....

....

....

MORNING JOURNALING

I am grateful for: ....

....

....

because ....

....

My focus/priorities for today: ....

....

....

....

....

EVENING JOURNALING

The best part of my day was ....

....

....

....

How did I get better or make someone better today? ....

....

....

....

MORNING JOURNALING

I am grateful for: ....

....

....

because ....

....

My focus/priorities for today: ....

....

....

....

....

EVENING JOURNALING

The best part of my day was ....

....

....

....

....

How did I get better or make someone better today? ....

....

....

....

MORNING JOURNALING

I am grateful for: ....

....

....

because ....

....

My focus/priorities for today: ....

....

....

....

....

EVENING JOURNALING

The best part of my day was ....

....

....

....

....

How did I get better or make someone better today? ....

....

....

....

If you have made it all the way through this journal, I'm seriously so proud of you. That is not easy and takes tons of discipline. I really hope you've learned a lot about yourself and been able to make some positive changes in your life. If you only did about half of it or fell a little short and forgot and want to start over again, I've got you covered.

For more space to write, start over, or if you are even looking to complete this journal for a second time through, maybe a second year in a row, **visit my website to download a printable version.**

www.saraglashagel.com

LET'S STAY CONNECTED!

Facebook.com/theroadtohappy.saraglashagel

Instagram.com/sara.glashagel

NOTES

Made in the USA
Coppell, TX
04 June 2021

56897525R00098